BACK TO BASICS

Gardening

Sue Phillips

Gardening

How to be a successful gardener, even if you've never done it before.

Sue Phillips

Abbeydale Press

Published by Abbeydale Press
An imprint of Bookmart Limited
Registered Number 2372865
Trading as Bookmart Limited
Desford Road
Enderby
Leicester LE9 5AD

ISBN 1-86147-018-5

Produced for Bookmart by Ideas into Print,
New Ash Green, Kent DA3 8JD

Colour reproduction by CK Litho Ltd,
Whitstable, Kent CT5 3PS

Printed in Spain

Below: You can create a delightful cottage garden effect by teaming self-seeding verbascum and foxgloves with spreading perennials such as achillea that don't need to be divided too often. Plant everything close together to smother out weeds.

Contents

Above: The way to get plants to grow well for you is to give them the right conditions. Here, shuttlecock fern teams with Bowles' golden grass; both enjoy moist conditions and light, dappled shade.

Part One

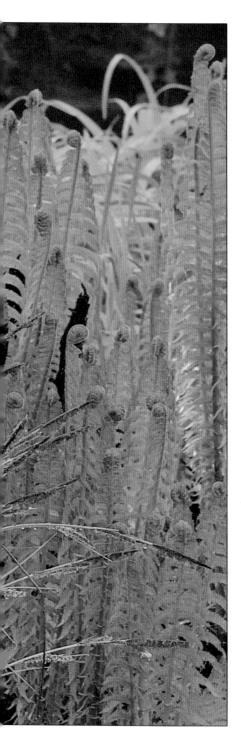

Making a practical start

Everyone has to start somewhere, so instead of worrying about what to do first or how to plan the garden, the best way to begin is just think about how you'd like the garden to look and get going! You don't need much equipment and there is no need to rip everything out and start from scratch. Clear up any rubbish, cut the grass and clip the hedge, then get out the worst of the weeds. With these basic tasks taken care of, any garden will look better straightaway. Then you can see what's worth keeping and start adding new features and plants of your own. Don't try to do the whole lot at once. Its easier – and much more fun – to let the garden 'grow up' round you gradually.

How plants grow – a bit of biology

Plants are like factories; from the outside they look relatively inactive, but there's a lot going on inside. Just like factories, plants take in various raw materials and use energy to turn them into other things, which they either store, use to expand their premises, or send out into the wider world.

THE NEXT GENERATION

The ultimate aim of any plant is to reproduce itself by shedding ripe seed. To produce a wide range of offspring, some of which may be better able to survive than others, many plants bear attractive flowers with pollen or nectar to attract insects that cross-pollinate them and so create new genetic combinations.

Sunlight
Sunlight provides the energy to drive the chemical processes involved in photosynthesis.

THE MANUFACTURING PROCESS

During daylight hours the green pigment chlorophyll traps sunlight and uses it as a source of energy to turn carbon dioxide from the air and water from the soil into carbohydrates. These are stored as starchy substances in the roots and leaves. This process is called photosynthesis.

Oxygen
Oxygen produced as a waste product of photosynthesis diffuses into the air from the leaves.

PLANT PHARMACY

Using basic raw ingredients (minerals, water and air), plants manufacture hormones that control the way different parts of the plant 'know' how to turn their tissues into roots, buds or leaves. Plants also make their own colouring materials, fragrances and a wide range of other sophisticated chemicals, including those that repel predators.

Carbon dioxide
Carbon dioxide used in photosynthesis is taken in through pores in the leaves.

NIGHT-TIME BREATHING

Plants respire rather like animals, taking in oxygen and giving off carbon dioxide. During the day, more carbon dioxide is taken in during photosynthesis than is given out in respiration. During the night, photosynthesis ceases and so respiration is the only process going on.

Food
Forty or more different minerals are taken up in the water absorbed through the roots.

Scientific Stuff

- **F1 hybrid seeds** are produced by crossing two purebred strains. The same cross must be recreated each time to get more of the same type of seed. If you sow the seeds produced by F1 hybrid plants, the offspring won't all be identical – more like a collection of mongrels. That's why F1 seeds are so expensive and you get so few in the packet when you buy them.

- **Open-pollinated varieties** of flowers and vegetables are those that have been produced over many generations by selecting the best of the crop to cross, until they produce purebred offspring that are all identical. Seeds of open-pollinated varieties (those that don't have F1 written against them in the catalogues) are cheaper and you get more in the packet, which reflects how much easier they are to produce.

Evaporating water

Water constantly evaporates from tiny pores in the leaves – a process called transpiration. If a plant loses more water than it takes up from the soil, it starts to wilt. Plants will normally recover from this temporary wilting when you water them.

Distribution

Some plants have evolved highly sophisticated means of ensuring that their own offspring don't grow too close to home and thus compete for light, water and nutrients. For example, acer seeds are winged so that they spin away on the breeze; caper spurge has explosive seedpods that 'shoot' seeds across the garden; tasty fruit ensures that animals swallow the seeds of various plants and deposit them later, some distance away, along with their own supply of manure.

To save your own seed, grow open-pollinated (non-hybrid) varieties, choose the best two plants and just before the flowers open, put a muslin bag over their heads before the

bees can get to them. When the flowers open, hand-pollinate them using a fine brush to transfer pollen between different flowers of both plants. Cover them until the seeds start to set, so that there's no risk of cross-pollination by wind or insects.

Right: Rosehips provide birds with a tasty 'bribe' for transporting the seeds. Passing through the bird's digestive system helps to prepare them for the germination process.

CONSTRUCTION COMPANY

Plants make their own structure, laying down lignin (wood) to support tall constructions – such as trees and the woody stems of perennial plants, cabbage stalks, etc. – and cellulose to make cell walls to build new leaves and other structures.

Water

Water taken in by the roots provides the hydrogen and oxygen used in photosynthesis.

Garden Doctor

- The secret of growing plants well is to make sure that they always have everything they need: enough light and water, the full range of nutrients, and the right temperature. If any one thing is in short supply, the plant will survive but growth slows down until the shortage is made up.

- Plants that are under stress due to lack of water, high temperatures or low nutrient levels often respond by trying to set seed as quickly as possible before they die. That is why salad crops, such as lettuce, and some vegetables, such as celeriac, Florence fennel and celery, 'bolt' (run to seed) unless growing conditions are good. It explains why plants such as these need to grow without a check if they are to flourish in the garden.

Vital ingredients – soil

Soil may not look very glamorous, but it is the heart of the garden. It is like a supermarket supplying water, air and food to the plants growing in it, and it also gives roots something to grip onto, so that they can hold plants upright – anything right up to the size of a tree. To garden successfully, you need to know a bit about your soil, which varies from garden to garden. But you cannot take soil for granted – you need to look after it.

Dig for victory

Gardening isn't a natural activity. In the wild, you only find a limited range of plants growing in any particular area, whereas in a garden there are lots of plants, all with different requirements. In the wild, plants grow and die, then rot and return their goodness to the soil for other plants to live on. If the plants get eaten by animals, their goodness returns to the ground as manure. In a garden, we want to grow a huge number of different kinds of plants close together and have them all look perfect. We take a lot out of the ground by harvesting vegetables and keeping the garden tidy. Pruning roses, cutting grass and clearing away bedding plants and dead leaves means nutrients are being taken out of the soil. Because we are always planting new things, the soil needs to stay light and fluffy so that new roots can grow easily. As a result of the intense activity taking place, soil needs help, so gardeners cultivate it and use compost and fertilisers to replace what they take out of the ground.

Below: You can't dig in organic matter after plants have been put in, but you can spread it on top of the soil as a mulch. The worms will then mix it into the soil for you.

pH – The acid test

Soil may be acid, neutral or alkaline. Some plants prefer one or the other, although most popular garden plants are easy-going and grow in any kind except the extremes. Soil test kits are sold in garden centres for checking soil pH (the scale used to register acidity or alkalinity). It is a good idea to do this when you move to a new garden.

It is not easy to alter the pH of soil reliably; you can add lime to acid soil or sulphur chips to chalky soil, but this needs doing every year and you must check the pH regularly before retreating the soil. It is usually easier to grow what is naturally happy in your soil, and then grow anything that doesn't like it in pots filled with a suitable potting mixture.

Acid soil: pH 4 (very acid) to pH 6.5 (slightly acid). Ericaceous plants, such as rhododendron, heather and cranberries, do best in very acid soil.

Neutral soil: pH 7. Most plants, other than real lime-haters or lime-lovers, are happy here.

Alkaline soil: pH 7.5 (slightly alkaline) to pH 9 (very chalky). Gypsophila, pinks and scabious are happiest on very chalky soils. Other plants may suffer from mineral deficiencies.

Garden Doctor – What sort of soil do I have?

DOES IT dry out fast after rain; do puddles vanish quickly? Feel gritty when rubbed between the fingers? Look light-coloured, or resemble building sand?
DIAGNOSIS Sandy soil.
REMEDY Improve with plenty of organic matter.

DOES IT feel sticky when wet, go boggy in winter and do puddles last for ages? Dry out into hard lumps or crack open when it's dry?
DIAGNOSIS Clay soil.
REMEDY Improve with organic matter and gritty sand or bark chippings.

DOES IT dry out quickly after rain, look pale and stony, or maybe have a thin layer of soil over white crumbly rock?
DIAGNOSIS Chalky soil.
REMEDY Improve with organic matter.

DOES IT look like dark brown crumbs? Is it in an old garden that has been well cultivated for many years, or old grassland recently turned into a garden?
DIAGNOSIS Loamy soil, the best sort for gardening on.
REMEDY Maintain its natural fertility by good cultivation.

Rub soil between your fingers; if it feels gritty, it has a high proportion of sand and you can expect it to be well drained.

Left: Rhododendrons are lime-haters. In the garden, acid soil is essential; if your soil is not suitable, grow them in pots of ericaceous (lime-free) potting mix and use a liquid feed containing sequestered iron each spring.

Scientific Stuff

Soil is not dead. There is plenty going on underground, where you can't see it, but it is all essential to the smooth running of the garden.

● Soil contains billions of microscopic organisms. Some are beneficial bacteria that 'eat' plant and animal remains, turning them into plant food. Some are harmful fungal organisms that cause plant diseases. Digging plenty of garden compost and manure into the soil is a good way of adding extra beneficial bacteria, but don't put diseased plant remains on the compost heap, otherwise they will spread when you use the compost.

● Worms are good for the soil, as their burrows make tiny airways that let water drain away. Worms also pull dead leaves and other materials into their burrows, which break down and improve the soil.

● Soil needs to have air spaces between the particles, so that roots can breathe and surplus water can drain away. Digging helps to increase soil aeration by 'fluffing up' the texture; adding organic matter helps, too. On clay soil, where aeration is specially poor due to the tiny particles that make up the soil, digging in grit or bark chippings helps to open up the texture of the soil.

Testing your soil for pH

1 *Soil test kits consist of a plastic test tube with a cap and a capsule of chemical that will react with the soil and water mix to produce a colour change that you can compare to a chart.*

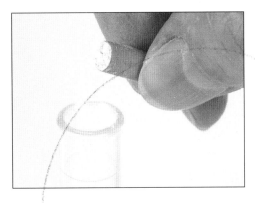

2 *Twist open the two halves of the capsule and pour the powder into the test tube. If necessary, use a fold of clean paper as a funnel to avoid spilling it.*

Hold the tube and the chart close together in good light over a white surface so that you clearly see the colours.

3 *Add some of your soil to the tube up to the first line and fill with water to the fourth line. Put the cap on and shake vigorously. Allow the contents to settle before comparing the colour.*

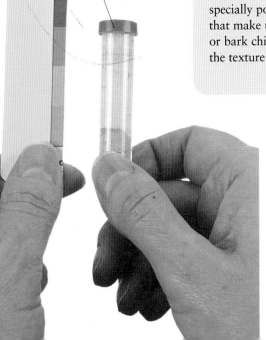

4 *Colour changes are never as definite as you might wish, but for this test kit the result shows the soil sample to be more acidic than it is alkaline. You can use an electronic meter if you need a more precise reading.*

Vital ingredients — water and watering

Although they look fairly solid, green plants are made up of more than 95% water. That's why they wilt when they are not watered. But water also provides plants with their own internal transport system, moving incoming nutrients and manufactured substances, such as carbohydrates and hormones, to wherever they are needed in order for the plants to survive, grow and reproduce themselves.

Plants don't get watered in the wild

In the wild, plants get by without any watering because wild plants grow from seeds that sprout where they land. As their roots are never dug up and damaged, they spread a long way in search of water, which makes them natural survivors. But they don't all grow into good-looking specimens; those that just manage to survive look very ragged, which isn't good enough for gardens.

In gardens, we don't want to grow the plants that appear naturally – weeds – we want manmade cultivars and exotic species from around the world, all of which have been artificially propagated, pricked out, potted or transplanted. Because their roots have been damaged by our interference, cultivated plants develop smaller, shallower root systems. And because they are growing away from their natural environment, they are never as robust as native species. However, we want them to grow stronger and look more attractive, and watering is one of the ways to help them do better.

Fit a rose to the spout of a watering can to water small seedlings with a fine shower.

Grandpa's Tip

In summer, water in the evenings so that plants have all night to 'drink' before the sun comes out and dries up moist soil. In winter, water in the morning – especially in the greenhouse – so that plants have a chance to dry off before it gets cold, otherwise they are more prone to attacks of mildew.

Keep separate watering cans for feeds and weedkillers to avoid accidents. Even washing out your weedkiller-can thoroughly won't get rid of every trace.

Below: A drip watering system is a sophisticated system for watering containers on the patio or in the greenhouse. Each plant has its own drip nozzle connected to a main water supply pipe. Timers attached to the tap automatically turn the water on and off at pre-set times.

Above: Small-scale sprinkler systems are one of several alternative types of irrigation suitable for vegetables and bedding plants, which need regular watering throughout the growing season.

WATERING TIPS

Not all plants need the same amount of watering. Here are some useful guidelines.

- **Water regularly**
Which? Plants in pots and other containers.
How? Fill containers to the rim with water and repeat until it just starts to trickle out through drainage holes in the bottom. Tip out saucers, so that plants are not left standing in water. Check plants in pots regularly and water them often enough so that the potting mix never dries out badly.

- **Water as soon as the soil starts to look or feel dry**
Which? Shallow-rooted plants, such as seasonal bedding plants, herbs, vegetables and salads.
How? Soak thoroughly, using a watering can, hosepipe or irrigation system.

- **Water after the top 2.5-5cm (1-2in) of soil dries out**
Which? Newly planted perennials, roses, trees, shrubs and climbers, including new hedges.
How? Soak the ground at the base of the plant once or twice a week with a hosepipe.

- **Water after several weeks of drought**
Which? Shallow-rooted shrubs, such as rhododendrons and camellias, and climbers growing on walls, as the soil always dries out quickest here.
How? Don't water little and often. Soak the plants thoroughly and repeat when necessary.

- **Don't bother watering**
Which? Established lawns, trees, shrubs and climbers, and hedges.
Why? It's much better to let their roots travel in search of water. If you start watering, roots grow up to the surface, which makes the plants less drought-resistant than before.

Left: Porous pipe is a good way to water vegetables. Lay a line along each row and turn the tap on for about 20 minutes every week. The water should spread for 30-45cm (12-18in) each side of the pipe, depending on the soil type, so space lengths of pipe accordingly.

Scientific Stuff – Adapted to cope

You can tell a lot about how to grow plants just by looking at them to see what they were used to 'back home' in the wild.

In hot dry areas where water is short, plants have evolved ways of saving it – waxy skin, furry leaves or silver coloration that reflects light. In deserts, many plants have given up leaves altogether and grow tough spines instead.

In damp, humid places, plants don't have to worry about saving water, so they have large, thin leaves. This is true of many bog garden plants and tropical houseplants.

Right: These are the clues that will tell you what conditions plants need to grow happily in the garden.

Drought-tolerant plants

Some herbs have silver foliage

Sempervivum has thick waxy leaves

Moisture-loving plants

Ferns have thin lacy leaves

Hostas have large thin leaves

Vital ingredients – plant foods and feeding

Plants get much of what they need from the soil, and from the compost and manure used to improve it, but in a crowded garden that is not enough. High-performance plants, such as long-flowering or heavy-cropping kinds, need extra feeding, and so do those growing in containers, where their roots can't spread far.

Recipes for success

Always keep a few basic plant feeds in stock. They last for years if stored somewhere cool, dry and dark, where they cannot freeze in winter.

Plants in the ground

Each spring, just as plants begin growing again, go round the whole garden sprinkling a general-purpose plant food or blood, fish and bone fertiliser over bare soil around shrubs, roses and perennials. Follow the rate recommended on the packet. If you drop fertiliser onto the leaves of a perennial plant, wash it off with plenty of water before it can scorch.

Above: When applying fertiliser don't exceed the recommended quantity and do spread it evenly. If the ground is dry, hoe the feed in lightly and water it well in.

Grandpa's Tip

Make your own manure tea – a health food drink for plants. Dunk a cloth bag filled with manure into a bucket of water until it turns the colour of strong tea, then dilute it with four times that amount of water. Use to water vegetables or tomatoes growing in the ground.

You can do the same with a bag of nettle tops, which make a high-nitrogen feed that is good for salad crops and herbs.

Plants in containers

Potting mixture contains some nutrients, but start feeding six weeks after planting into soil-less potting mix, or three months after planting into soil-based potting mix. Then begin feeding regularly once a week with any good brand of liquid or soluble feed, using the diluted feed in place of plain water when the plants need a drink. Stop feeding during the winter when plants are not growing.

Heavy-cropping plants

Heavy-cropping plants need 'topping up' with nutrients regularly during the growing season. These include vegetables, tomatoes and fruit bushes, and plants with a long flowering season, such as roses and bedding plants. Either water them fortnightly with diluted liquid feeds, or sprinkle general-purpose fertiliser round them every four weeks and water it well in.

Left: A perennial border like this needs feeding in late spring just before plants start growing. A summer feed is optional, but worth doing on hungry sandy soil. Use a general-purpose fertiliser and make sure that the soil is moist, so that the fertiliser dissolves into the film of water around the soil particles, enabling the plant roots to absorb it.

TYPES OF PLANT FOOD

• **Liquid and soluble feeds** are taken up instantly by plants, and are the safest feeds to use in pots and other containers, as the nutrients are already in liquid form when you apply them. There are two basic types. General-purpose liquid or soluble feeds contain a higher proportion of nitrogen than anything else, so use them for foliage plants. High-potash tomato feeds are for 'fruiting' crops, such as peppers, as well as for tomatoes. Diluted to a quarter or half the usual strength, you can also use them to feed free-flowering plants, such as tuberous begonias and fuchsias.

Above: Measure liquid feeds out carefully and use them at the recommended rate. Feed little and often for the best results.

• **General-purpose granular and powder fertilisers** are the cheapest sort for general use all round the garden. Use them in spring or when preparing the ground before planting. Don't use them in containers, as there's a risk of scorching the roots.

• **Specialist feeds** are available for plants such as roses, ericaceous (lime-hating) plants, lawns, etc. They provide precisely the right blend of nutrients for those plants.

• **Slow-release feeds** are handy if you forget to liquid-feed pots, tubs and hanging baskets regularly. With many brands, a single dose mixed into the potting mixture at planting time is enough to last the rest of the season. Feed sticks do the same sort of thing, although they don't always last as long. Push them in close to the roots.

• **Organic feeds** contain ingredients with natural origins that organic gardeners prefer to use instead of synthetic fertilisers. You can buy organic versions of a good range of granular fertilisers and liquid feeds. The plants don't really notice the difference, but organic products are more likely to contain a good range of trace elements, which enthusiasts claim improve both flavour and colour.

Above: Feed 'sticks' are a handy way of feeding plants in containers. Just push in the required number round the edge of the pot.

• **Seaweed extracts** are growth stimulants that don't supply the plant with its main nutrients, but are good for topping up trace elements. Use them in addition to normal feeds, especially for salads, vegetables, seedlings and young plants, long-term plants in pots and containers, and anything in need of a boost.

Above: Foliar feed is quickly taken up by plants, but don't spray in hot sunny weather. You can reapply them frequently.

• **Foliar feeds** are sprayed onto the leaves and are quickly taken in, making them good tonics for sickly plants and newly propagated plants without much root. Foliar feeds are used at very weak dilution rates to avoid scorching foliage.

• **Iron tonics, or sequestered iron feeds,** are used for lime-hating plants such as rhododendrons, where they are growing on soil that is insufficiently acid. In this situation, iron is 'locked up' in the soil, so the leaves start turning yellow. A single dose each spring usually does the trick. It's also good for lime-hating plants grown in pots.

Scientific Stuff – What's on the menu?

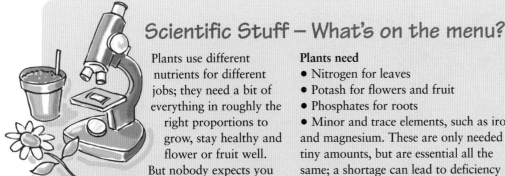

Plants use different nutrients for different jobs; they need a bit of everything in roughly the right proportions to grow, stay healthy and flower or fruit well. But nobody expects you to be a chemist, which is why most fertilisers and liquid feeds contain a balance of all the main nutrients. Some products also contain many of the minor nutrients and trace elements, but these are also found in soil, garden compost and fertilisers from natural origins.

Plants need
• Nitrogen for leaves
• Potash for flowers and fruit
• Phosphates for roots
• Minor and trace elements, such as iron and magnesium. These are only needed in tiny amounts, but are essential all the same; a shortage can lead to deficiency symptoms on very acid or very chalky soil.

Right: Roses and clematis are naturally heavy feeders and need regular feeding throughout the growing season. A tangle of climbers growing through each other on the same support need specially generous treatment.

What you need – tools and equipment

You don't need to buy a lot of expensive equipment to get gardening; a few basic tools are fine to start with. In time, a few more bits and pieces make gardening easier and more convenient, but they aren't essential. And you can hire equipment, such as a rotavator, that you only need occasionally.

Spade for digging and for planting trees and shrubs.

Garden fork for breaking up soil and spreading organic matter.

Trowel (or hand fork) for planting small plants and hand weeding.

Hoe for fast weeding without kneeling down.

Rake for smoothing soil before sowing, for gathering up leaves and rubbish and for levelling gravel paths.

MIGHT-LIKE-TO-HAVE TOOLS

Secateurs, for cutting back shrubs and routine pruning.

Wheelbarrow, for moving heavy loads around the garden.

Gardening gloves. Use heavy-duty ones for protection against thorns, etc., when pruning roses or prickly shrubs or clearing rough ground; lightweight, water-resistant gloves when weeding and potting; rubber gloves when mixing chemicals or spraying.

A hosepipe saves time when you have a lot of watering to do, but install an outdoor tap to save threading the end indoors through the kitchen window.

Above: Use secateurs for all garden snipping and cutting jobs. Some models have a notch in the base of the blades for cutting wire.

Cost cutter

Don't spend a lot of money on expensive stainless steel garden tools – yet. Choose a budget range from a top-named manufacturer. The best buy stainless steel tool is a trowel.

Alternatively, consider a range of tools that are sold as separate heads and handles. This way you can buy only what you need to start with and gradually add to it. You can also choose different handle lengths to suit every member of the family.

Watering can for watering and liquid feeding plants in containers.

Wheelbarrow for moving soil, compost and manure around the garden and taking weedy rubbish to the compost heap. Alternatively, use a large builder's bucket.

16

CHOOSING A LAWN MOWER

Nowadays, not all gardens have a lawn, but if you do have one, you'll need to cut it regularly. However, there's no need to invest in a huge petrol mower or expensive ride-on model – choose one that's the right size and price for the job. A cutting width of 25-30cm (10-12in) is plenty for small gardens, and means the mower is light enough for less hefty members of the family to use.

Hover mowers

Electric hover mowers float on a cushion of air, so as well as mowing backwards and forwards, you can also go sideways and right over the edge of beds, which can be handy. Larger models have grass collection boxes, but small ones leave the clippings on the lawn. This is no problem if you cut the grass before it gets too long, as the clippings soon disappear. Otherwise, you need to rake up the grass afterwards to stop it turning to 'hay' or treading indoors.

Electric rotary mowers

These inexpensive mowers for small gardens have a wheel at each corner, which makes them lighter to push but less manoeuvrable. Don't use electric mowers on wet grass.

Rotary motor mowers

Although expensive, these more powerful mowers are capable of tackling longer grass, even when it's wet. A petrol mower is essential in a large garden that is too long for an electric cable to reach. They need more storage space and annual servicing.

Cylinder mowers

These are essential for traditional stripes. Motor versions are expensive and need a lot of maintenance. Hand versions are ideal for tiny lawns if you can find one; they sometimes turn up in secondhand shops.

Recycler mowers

This is a special type of rotary motor mower that chops up even long grass very finely and blasts it down into the turf so you don't need to empty grass boxes. More expensive than normal rotary mowers.

Robot mowers

The lazy gardener's friend, robot mowers can be programmed to cut the grass as often as you like, even when you aren't there. Initially expensive, the price is coming down all the time as the technology gets cheaper.

Above: When using an electric mower, always loop the cable up over your shoulder, so that there is no risk of cutting the cable. Plug the mower into a circuit breaker, for safety.

Choosing a hoe

Garden centres sell a bewildering range of hoes; don't be afraid to try out several different kinds on their carpet to see if the weight, handle length and working action are right for you.

Draw hoe. Use with a chopping action to cut down larger weeds when clearing soil. Also good for weeding between straight rows of vegetables.

Two-bladed hoes. Various unusual-looking hoes are available, with cutting blades on both front and back edges. These are used with a push-pull action and halve the job of weeding, as they scythe down weeds on both strokes.

Dutch hoe. Push the tip of the blade along, just below the surface of the soil, to slice weeds from their roots. Best for annual weeds in borders before they get too big.

Storage

There's no need to clutter up a small garden with a shed; instead, hang tool racks on the inside walls of the garage to store basic implements. Small hover and electric rotary mowers also lay flat for storing this way. Alternatively, buy a garden store, which is a large, lockable box, big enough to take basic tools, a small mower and some garden seats, leaving a flat top that doubles as a plant display stand or buffet table top when you are having a barbecue.

Grandpa's Tip

Stick coloured tape around the handles of trowels, secateurs and other small items that are easily lost if you put them down in the garden, so they show up well. After use, clean garden tools with a stiff brush or damp cloth to remove soil, then wipe them with an oily rag or spray them with aerosol oil to prevent rusting. Hang them on a rack inside the shed or garage where they are always easy to find.

The right plant for the right garden

The art of good gardening lies in knowing what to plant where. It is quite easy to find out what individual plants need – for example, sun or shade, damp or well-drained soil – as you'll find the information on the back of the label when you buy them, or you can look it up in reference books. It is harder to 'see' the growing conditions in different parts of your garden from a plant's point of view, so you need to do a bit of detective work. It's worth the effort; if you match plants to places properly, they literally grow themselves and you avoid lots of problems. It'll also save you a fortune!

The first thing to do is to assess your growing conditions. They may vary between one end of the garden and the other. You need to establish the following:

Your soil type See page 10-11.

The pH of the soil See page 10-11.

The general conditions Is the garden shady and damp? Open and windswept? Sheltered and sunny? Hot and dry? Is yours a particularly mild or cold region? Or is the garden at the bottom of a dip or slope so that frost lasts late into winter mornings (a frost pocket)?

Aspect From which direction does the garden receive most of its light? If it is on a slope, which direction does that face? If a garden is flanked by tall trees or buildings that prevent light reaching all or part of it from one direction, it is said to face the direction from which it receives most light.

Sunlight hours How much sun does any particular area receive during the day? One to two hours, roughly half the day, all day?

It can be very helpful to draw a plan of the garden, mark in north and south, and use colours to show the areas that are fully shaded (for instance by buildings), or receive dappled shade under trees, or sun for half the day, or all day. Then you can see at a glance what growing conditions are like all round the garden. This will help when buying plants and deciding what to grow where. Take a copy of the plan to the garden centre when you go shopping.

Below: Rhododendrons, heathers and conifers are naturally 'at home' in a garden on acid soil, though many non acid-loving plants, such as daffodils, also thrive in these conditions.

Grandpa's Tip

Weeds are a good way to tell how fertile (or otherwise) the soil is. If nettles grow big and strong there's plenty of nitrogen. If weeds are weak and stunted, the soil is poor; if they are big, green, fast-growing and leafy it's probably quite fertile. If your garden soil looks dark in colour compared to surrounding fields, etc., this shows that it has been well cultivated over the years and contains plenty of organic matter.

CHALKY SOIL
Shrubs: Buddleja, flowering cherry, crab apples, forsythia, hardy fuchsia, phlomis, potentilla.
Perennials: Gypsophila, pinks, scabious.

CLAY SOIL
Shrubs: Berberis, cornus, corylus, miscanthus, roses, salix, *Sambucus nigra* cultivars.
Perennials, etc: Bluebells, cultivated celandines (*Ranunculus ficaria* cultivars), daffodils, *Houttuynia cordata* 'Chameleon', *Phalaris arundinacea* 'Picta' (gardener's garters grass).

EXPOSED WINDY GARDEN
Trees and shrubs: Berberis, birch, chaenomeles, cotoneaster, elaeagnus, hawthorns, heathers, *Rosa rugosa*, *Sorbus aucuparia* (mountain ash, rowan), symphoricarpos.

LIME-FREE (ACID) SOIL
Shrubs: Abies, *Acer palmatum* cultivars, camellia, crinodendron, gaultheria, heathers (except winter-flowering), magnolia, picea, pieris, pinus, rhododendron, witch hazel.

SEASIDE GARDEN
Shrubs: Atriplex, *Elaeagnus* x *ebbingei*, escallonia, double-flowered gorse, *Hebe salicifolia*, hippophae, *Pinus nigra maritima*, *Pinus radiata*, senecio, tamarix.

Important

Most popular garden plants are very easy-going and will grow in a wide range of sites and situations, so if you do have a 'problem' spot don't worry about it – most widely available plants will grow there successfully.

Above: A damp, shady garden is perfectly suited to moisture-loving foliage plants, such as hosta, gunnera and hardy ferns. Flowering bog plants mostly prefer a sunnier spot, but arum lily (shown here) is fine for light shade.

A WALL FACING THE SUN

A premium site for 'special' sunloving or slightly tender climbers or wall-trained shrubs.

Climbers: Campsis, passionflower, *Solanum crispum*, trachelospermum.
Fruit: Apricots, figs, nectarines and peaches.
Wall shrubs: Ceanothus, *Cytisus battandieri* (pineapple broom), fremontodendron, *Magnolia grandiflora*, phygelius.

A WALL FACING AWAY FROM THE SUN

A traditionally difficult site that you can bring to life with the right planting.
Climbers: Ivies, *Clematis* 'Nelly Moser', climbing rose 'Danse du Feu'.
Wall-trained shrubs: Camellia, *Cotoneaster horizontalis, Crinodendron hookerianum*, euonymus, *Garrya elliptica, Hydrangea petiolaris, Jasminum nudiflorum* (winter jasmine).

GARDEN WITH SUN LATER IN THE DAY

Good for early-flowering shrubs and plants that like good light but don't want over-strong sun. These gardens are good for sitting in after work, as they enjoy the evening sun, so this is a good place for growing plants in containers.
Climbers: Clematis.
Containers: Begonias, fuchsias, petunias.
Shrubs: Camellia, chaenomeles (ornamental quince).

Above: Plants that enjoy similar growing conditions, such as these sunlovers, naturally 'look right' together, which makes it much easier to plan a good-looking garden.

Above: The vast majority of perennial flowers will be happy in a situation where they get direct sun for at least half the day.

GARDEN WITH SUN IN THE MORNING

Avoid early-flowering shrubs and fruit, as blossoms are likely to be damaged by rapid warming following late frosts. This results in poor fruit set and browning flowers.
Climbers: *Celastrus scandens*, late-flowering clematis, such as viticella varieties, late Dutch honeysuckle, *Jasminum officinale*, parthenocissus.
Shrubs: *Cotoneaster horizontalis, Kerria japonica*, pyracantha.

A GARDEN FACING THE SUN

Very sunny, but can be dry, especially on a slope facing the sun.
Climbers: Grapevines, climbing roses.
Mediterranean herbs: Bay, lavender, rosemary, coloured sages, thyme.
Perennials: Acanthus, achillea, alstroemeria, artemisia, eryngium.
Rock plants: Sedum, sempervivum.
Sunloving shrubs: Buddleja, cytisus (broom), genista, hebe, myrtle, romneya.

19

Improving your existing plants

Don't assume that plants will automatically grow into an attractive shape all on their own. Left to grow 'naturally', some kinds often get themselves into quite a mess. Fortunately, there are several easy ways of improving on nature. And before buying, give any plant a quick look-over, to make sure you come away with a good buy. You will soon see that some are better than others.

Pruning a lopsided shrub

Remove branches that spoil the shape, cutting them off close to the base of the plant or where they join a main stem. When new shoots start to grow, leave those that balance up the shape and remove any that lean out the wrong way.

Renovating an old shrub

When old shrubs become unproductive and tatty, cut out two or three of the oldest branches as close to the base of the plant as you can in spring. Repeat this each year until all the old stems have been replaced by vigorous new ones. Don't cut back the whole shrub in one go, as it may not flower for years if you do.

Stopping

This is done to make young plants and newly potted cuttings grow bushier. Nip out the growing tip of a shoot using finger and thumbnails in a pinching action; this makes several sideshoots appear at the end of the stem. If you want a big bushy plant, wait till the sideshoots are 5cm (2in) long, then nip out their tips so the sideshoots in turn grow sideshoots. However, each time you 'stop' a plant, you delay flowering by several weeks, so it is best done early in the season.

Clipping and trimming

Done regularly to maintain the shape of topiary, cloud-trimmed conifers, climbers trained over wire frameworks, box finials and similar plant shapes. Sheep shears or kitchen scissors are the handiest tool for working on small plants. Slow-growing plants such as box need trimming twice a year, but fast-growing *Lonicera nitida* may need tidying up every six weeks throughout the summer.

Right place, wrong plant

It's tempting to keep cutting back a big or fast-growing shrub that blocks the path or overhangs steps, but all this does is make it grow faster, and the strong young growth may not flower. In this case it is far better to remove the plant entirely and replace it with something smaller and slower-growing that won't become a nuisance.

Left: Box is easy to train. Choose a strong, bushy young plant or rooted cutting, trim it roughly to shape and every time new growth is about 2.5cm (1in) long, clip off the tips as you form the shape.

Above: There are two distinct types of fuchsia: the upright, bushy sort (above), and trailing types. Use upright ones to train into standards, and trailing types for hanging baskets.

Above: When stopping a cutting, only remove the very tip of the shoot, just above a pair of leaves. Sideshoots will soon start growing.

Pinching out

You can control the eventual shape of plants by pinching out the tips of shoots to make them grow bushier, or by removing unwanted shoots completely while they are small. This is very useful for plants whose natural tendency is to grow a few long stems (such as some varieties of fuchsia), when you want to turn them into standard plants. These look like lollipops – a sphere growing on top of a tall, straight stem.

CHECK OUT THE FOLLOWING WHEN BUYING NEW PLANTS

• **The name** If the plant is in flower, does it look like the picture on the label? If it is not in flower, and the plant looks different from the rest of the batch, it may have been wrongly labelled.

• **Best varieties** If you are not familiar with particular plants, always choose varieties that have been given merit awards – they are usually the best available. Look for the symbols on the labels. If in doubt, ask for advice from a salesperson.

• **Health and condition** Orange spots, black or brown leaves may indicate disease. Broken stems and leaves may indicate careless handling, which in turn may mean plants have not been well cared for. Weeds, moss or liverwort growing in the pots is often a sign that plants have been in stock for a long time and may be in need of feeding. Poor-quality plants can be improved in time, but why waste your money? Choose good, healthy, vigorous ones that don't create problems and that look good in the garden from day one.

• **Shape** A badly shaped plant can be improved, but it takes months or even years of pruning, so it makes sense to choose a good specimen that earns its keep in the garden straightaway.

Trees Look for a single trunk with no branches for about 60cm/24in from the ground (bush tree); 90cm/36in (half standard) or 120cm/48in (full standard). A young tree may have 'feathers' growing out from the trunk. Cut these off, leaving a straight stem up to the crown, where the branches spread out. Look for five or more strong stems branching out evenly all round. A tree with only a few branches on one side will always look lopsided.

Shrubs Choose shrubs with five or more shoots growing out evenly from the base. Poorly shaped shrubs are much easier to correct than badly shaped trees, but you will still lose a season's

growth. Avoid shrubs where there appear to be two different types of shoots growing from the same plant, as these will be grafted plants where some suckers are growing up from the rootstock. Unless regularly removed, suckers will 'take over' from the plant you really wanted.

Bad plant: This is exactly the same variety of spiraea as the plant on the right, but look at the difference. This one is lanky and shapeless, with little new growth coming from the base, which will make it look increasingly leggy unless something is done about it.

Good plant: This is a much better buy – a compact plant, with dense foliage, plenty of shoots growing out from the base and a neat, symmetrical shape. It will grow into a well-shaped shrub.

Correcting a lopsided shrub

1 *If there is no alternative but to buy a poorly shaped shrub, you can improve it by hard pruning, but you'll most likely miss a season's flowering. Be bold!*

Deutzia x hybrida 'Pink Pompon'

2 *Trim back all the shoots to 15cm (6in) from the top of the pot; cut weak stems back a bit more and strong stems a bit less, leaving the plant a nice, even shape.*

Basic garden design tips

Designing a brand new garden or giving an old one a makeover isn't as difficult as you might think. The first job can be divided into three main phases: making decisions, doing a design and then actually doing the work. But the good news is, it doesn't all have to be done at once. Unless you are in a hurry, it makes sense to stagger both the work and the expense over several years, completing one phase at a time.

Above: Traditional gardens are more flower-packed and generally suit keener gardeners. Here, the colourful effect has been achieved by 'bedding out' standard fuchsias and pelargoniums for the summer.

Left: Container gardens are ideal for really tiny plots or those that have been paved over and have few beds to grow plants in. To reduce the workload, use plenty of big tubs planted with compact shrubs that can be left in the same pots for several years, instead of annual bedding plants that need to be replaced on a regular basis.

The planning process

Decisions
Ask yourself which plants and features you want to keep of the old garden. How will it be used in the future? Who will use it? What special features should it include?

Planning
Choose a way of working that suits you. The options are to:
1. Draw an overhead plan on squared paper.
2. Make models and move them round a paper garden shape.
3. Use a garden design programme on the computer. Various CD-roms are available, some of which include a plant encyclopedia.

Paper or model method

1 Make a scale drawing. Mark in the house, showing the windows and doors. Show the boundaries and features you plan to keep, such as trees, a shed, a pond, etc.

2 Lay a sheet of tracing paper over your scale drawing or make models to stand on it, and use this to try out various arrangements of beds, borders, patio or decking, and other key features within the garden. Keep moving things round and altering the shapes they make together until you are happy with the result.

3 Come up with three good ideas, all completely different, then compare them and see which you like best. Take your time; you'll have to live with the end result for quite a few years.

4 Prepare lists of materials for hard projects, such as paving, and work out a planting plan for your beds so you know what you need to buy and have an idea of costs.

5 If you want to be really professional about it, prioritise the work, starting with the most important features, and schedule the various jobs into a calendar.

Above: Winter is the time most people choose to try out new ideas for rearranging the garden, as there is not much work to do outside.

Grandpa's Tip

If you don't know what you want, there's no better way of picking up ideas than by visiting other people's gardens. Visit national shows and garden centres with demonstration gardens. Watch the television makeover programmes and look in books of garden plans. You don't have to copy other people's ideas exactly, but they are often a good starting point; adapt them to suit yourself and your garden.

DESIGNER TRICKS OF THE TRADE

• Make the most of a long, narrow garden or other odd-shaped plot by dividing it up into several 'garden rooms' using trellis, arches, tall borders, dwarf hedges or paths. One big advantage of this is that you can develop each area with a character of its own, so you could have, say, a seaside garden, a herb garden, and a lawn.

• Arrange the garden so that you have attractive views from the house, but so that you don't just look straight to the bottom of the garden. You should still have to go outside to 'explore' it all.

• Use plenty of evergreens to create the basic shape of the garden, which lasts all year round. Evergreens are also useful for hiding a bad view, creating privacy if the garden is overlooked or screening out electricity pylons and other eyesores.

• Before committing yourself, lay out the rough shape of your new plan in the existing garden, outlining a patio with paving slabs, and beds with a hosepipe or by trickling sand onto the grass. You can also stand pots of plants roughly in place. Then take a look out of the upstairs windows and keep moving everything around until you are happy with the result.

Right: A sloping garden can be terraced to make a series of mini gardens leading into each other, as they have done in this small town garden. As well as looking attractive, it makes the best use of the space.

Above: Contemporary styles rely on strong shapes, and materials such as gravel, pebbles, mirrors and trellis for their character. You don't need many plants, but those you do have need to be 'architectural', such as phormium, yucca or ornamental grasses and bamboos.

Right: Family gardens should have plenty of grass to play on, paving for a barbecue and sun loungers, and borders of resilient shrubs that grow back quickly and don't have thorns or sharp leaves. Avoid fragile or fussy flowers, or anything poisonous. Play areas such as sandpits can be restyled as the family grows up and made into planting beds.

Getting the ground ready to use

Digging is the best way to improve the condition of the soil. When digging over a new bed, you have an ideal opportunity to remove weeds and their roots, and to add plenty of bulky organic matter, such as decayed plant remains or animal manure, plus fertiliser. Each time you remove one 'crop' of plants, dig in more organic matter and plant food to replace what has been taken out, ready for the next crop. If you skimp on this vital preparation, fertility declines and garden plants will not grow well – but weeds will.

Anatomy of a digging campaign

✗ Weeds
Annual weeds compete with plants for water and nutrients, and can harbour pests and diseases. Perennial weeds can smother or strangle garden plants, as well as ruining the look of the garden.

✔ Organic matter
The vital 'roughage' that improves soil texture, making it porous and spongy so that it holds water but the surplus can drain away after rain. Also creates air spaces and retains moisture, so that roots thrive. Breaks down to humus, releasing natural nutrients and helping beneficial soil bacteria.

✔ Fertiliser
Replaces the main nutrients that are removed by high-yielding plants, such as vegetables.

All about glyphosate

Glyphosate weedkiller is ideal for clearing new ground before planting, because as well as killing annual weeds, it also kills perennials, roots and all. The product is best applied using a watering can fitted with a trickle bar or coarse rose. Keep a separate can for weedkiller, as you can never really wash out every trace. Glyphosate weedkillers are taken in through green leaves and move down inside the plant. Although at first it doesn't look as if anything is happening, don't be fooled. Weeds eventually start to dry out and turn brown, and after six weeks they can be dug in. Very well-established clumps of tough perennial weeds may sometimes start to regrow, in which case give them a second dose when they have come through about 2.5cm (1in). Glyphosate can't tell the difference between weeds and plants you might want to keep; it kills anything green, so cover plants to be spared and don't spray when it's windy or the drift can harm nearby plants. Since glyphosate doesn't harm the soil, it is safe to replant by the time the weeds have been killed.

Below: A completely untouched piece of ground needs clearing first. Remove brambles and rubble, then kill off grass and perennial weeds using a glyphosate-based weedkiller. Wait until the weeds are dead before digging the area. While you are waiting, prune overgrown shrubs, repair fences and treat them with timber preservative.

The no-dig technique

Once you have prepared the ground properly to make a new bed or border, you don't have to dig it again. Let the worms do the hard work for you. Here's how.

Don't step on the soil; it compacts it down, which stops water running away easily and makes it harder for plant roots to penetrate and develop properly. Hoe and plant from the edges of the bed instead.

In early spring, while the ground is moist, spread 2.5-5cm (1-2in) of well-rotted organic matter all over any bare soil as a mulch. Alternatively, use bark chippings, which cost more and break down more slowly, but last longer and are better at smothering out weeds.

Hoe off weeds while they are small so that they shrivel up on the spot.

Reapply more mulching materials every spring. Put in new plants if required, through the layer of new mulching material.

Grandpa's Tip

People often think it's going to be much easier to use a rotavator than to dig ground over with a spade. But rotavators are not as easy to use as they look; you need to press down hard on the handles to make them bite into the ground instead of just running along on top, and a big, powerful model can easily 'run away' with you. If the soil is too dry or too wet, a rotavator doesn't do much good, and if there are perennial weed roots in the ground, a rotavator just chops them up. With problem weeds, such as couch grass, ground elder and bindweed, each little piece grows and turns into a new plant. As a rule, unless the ground is in good condition and free from perennial weeds, digging is easier and does a better job.

Preparing new ground from scratch

1 *If you want to plant straightaway, strip off a layer of turf 2.5cm (1in) thick to remove all roots. Alternatively, water it with a glyphosate-based weedkiller and wait six weeks. Then dig in the dead grass.*

2 *Dig over the ground, incorporating as much well-rotted organic matter as possible to improve the soil. On clay soil, dig in one bucketful of gritty sand per square metre/yard as well, to prevent the soil setting solid in hot weather and to improve drainage when it is wet.*

3 *If possible, prepare new ground in autumn and leave it rough through the winter, so that the birds can clear up soil pests for you. Fork it over occasionally to turn up those pests hiding underground.*

Preparing previously cultivated soil for planting

1 *Shortly before planting, spread a thin layer of well-rotted organic matter over the surface and sprinkle general-purpose fertiliser evenly over the area at the rate recommended on the packet.*

2 *Fork over the ground, removing any weeds and roots as you go, and turning the compost and fertiliser in. It is perfectly OK to bury annual weeds when digging, as long as they have not yet seeded.*

3 *Rake the ground roughly level, removing any stones and roots. If you are preparing the ground for sowing seeds, then rake it extra well, leaving the soil looking like cake crumbs.*

Above: Putting plants together is an art – but it comes with practice. Create contrasts of shape and texture, but make sure that all the plants need the same growing conditions. This group is growing in a hot, dry, sunny gravel garden.

Part Two

Grow almost anything

People say you need 'green fingers' to be a gardener, but there is really no great mystery to it. The secret is matching the plant to the place. Before buying, check how big your plant will grow, and the soil and situation it prefers, then plant it – properly – in the right spot. Once it is in, don't just forget about it. If the weather is dry, new plants need regular watering until their roots have gone out into the ground and are properly established, which can take several months. If you are new to gardening, it makes sense to start with easy plants and leave the tricky ones until you've had some practice. Just ask for help when you go to buy, if you aren't sure which are which!

Plant it right

It doesn't take long to plant things properly, and it is worth doing as it plays such an important part in getting new plants off to a good start. Hurried planting or inadequate soil preparation can mean that plants don't grow well; they can even stay in 'suspended animation' for years after planting. It's not unknown for people to plant shrubs without first taking off the pot!

When to plant hardy plants

Although you can plant potgrown shrubs, etc., at any time of year when the soil is workable – even when they are in flower – the very best planting times are:
Conifers and evergreens: Mid-spring and early autumn. **Woody trees, shrubs, fruit and climbers:** Autumn. **Hardy perennials and rock plants:** Spring.

When to plant frost-tender plants

Tender plants include slightly tender perennials and shrubs (many of these are more tender than usual while they are young); half-hardy annuals (summer bedding and patio plants); frost-tender herbs and vegetables, including tomatoes, courgettes, aubergine and basil. Watch the

Above: If you don't have a cold frame or greenhouse in which to harden off tender bedding plants, it is usually much better to leave them in the garden centre until after the last frost in your area. Once trays of bedding and patio plants are displayed outdoors there, you can be perfectly certain that it is safe to plant them out in your garden.

Right: When you plant a tree, hammer in a short stake alongside it at an angle of about 45°, with the tip about 30cm (12in) from the base of the tree. That way, there is no risk of the tip impaling the rootball. Fix the trunk to the stake using a proper tree tie. Always tie the tree to the stake, not the stake to the tree.

Clematis

Lavender

Bearded iris

weather and don't plant these until just after the last frost, in late spring or early summer. If you've recently moved to a new area, nurserymen and keen gardeners will know when it's safe to plant, so ask them or wait until you see them do their planting.

Hardening off tender plants

If you buy plants that are not hardy, such as bedding plants, before the last frost, make sure you can stand them somewhere safe, such as a greenhouse, car port or sunroom. Harden them off for 10-14 days before planting them in the garden to accustom them gradually to outdoor conditions. To do this, stand them outside during the day and bring them in again at night. If you have a cold frame or cloches, you can stand them under those and remove the lid every day, replacing it again at night.

PLANTING DEPTH

As a good general rule, put in new plants so that the top of the rootball is level with the surrounding soil. However, there are some exceptions. With bearded irises, the top half of the rhizomes should be above the ground after planting. Clematis need planting deeply, with the top of the rootball 10-15cm (4-6in) down, so they can send out new shoots from underground stems if they are damaged by careless hoeing or clematis wilt disease.

Grandpa's Tip

Don't skimp on your soil preparation. Spend as much time making the hole as you do choosing the plant. Dig a big hole, mix in plenty of compost and some fertiliser, unless you're planting in autumn or winter. That way, there's a much better chance of your plant surviving and doing well.

Planting a shrub

If the potting mixture is dry, stand the plant (in its pot) overnight in a bucket containing about 15cm (6in) of water, for a good soak before planting.

1 *Prepare the planting area well. If you are planting a new border, prepare the soil as described on page 25. If you are just putting an individual plant into an existing border, dig a hole about twice the size of the pot and take a bucketful of well-rotted organic matter, such as garden compost. Tip half into the bottom of the hole and stir it into the soil with a fork. Then mix the other half with the soil you removed from the hole, ready to use later on.*

2 *Take the plant out of its pot. If it doesn't lift out easily, bang the base of the pot down sharply on a hard surface to loosen the rootball. If you cannot remove the pot because thick roots are growing out through the drainage holes in the base, carefully cut away the pot.*

3 *Take a look at the rootball. If it is packed solid, gently uncoil several of the largest roots from round the base, otherwise they will have difficulty growing out into the soil.*

4 *Using the empty pot as a guide, check that the planting hole is the right depth. The surface of the rootball should lie level with the surrounding soil. Stand the plant in place and turn it round until its best side faces the front of the border. Use the soil/compost mixture prepared earlier to fill the gap between the sides of the rootball and the edge of the planting hole.*

Important

Be sure to water the plant very thoroughly after planting it. This washes the soil down around the roots so that they are surrounded by soil and not air pockets, which they could not grow into.

Visit the new plant regularly and keep it well watered until it is established and you can see that it is growing happily. Plants put in during autumn normally need little or no extra watering, as the weather takes care of it for you. Anything planted in late spring or summer may need watering regularly throughout the summer.

5 *Use your heel to firm the soil down gently; don't trample on it. Water the new plant thoroughly and spread a generous layer of mulching material around it. Keep it watered in dry spells until it is properly established. You'll know when this has happened, because the plant will start to grow more vigorously.*

29

Planning a mixed border

Mixed borders contain a bit of everything – trees, shrubs, roses, evergreens, flowers and bulbs – so that they remain colourful all year round. However, you need quite a large area to fit in so many different plants. In a small garden you can make a small mixed border if you leave out the trees and use only smaller shrubs, such as hebes, and compact patio or groundcover roses, plus flowers.

ALTERNATIVE BORDERS

You don't have to choose a traditional mixed border. By varying the mixture of plants used, you can create a particular style to suit your taste.

Herbaceous border
A traditional blend of summer-flowering perennials, such as delphiniums, gypsophila, lupins, phlox and stachys.

Subtropical border
Tender or exotic-looking plants, such as banana plant, canna, castor oil plant, gazania, phygelius and shrubby salvias.

Cottage garden border
Old-fashioned flowers (including hardy annuals such as nasturtiums), herbs, campanula, Canterbury bells, foxgloves, lavender, roses, sweet williams.

Rose border
Standard roses, bush roses, compact patio and/or groundcover roses, underplanted with contrasting foliage or flowers.

Spring border
Spring bulbs, early-flowering shrubs and early perennials such as brunnera.

Above: In a cottage-style border, small spreading and self-seeding plants, such as diascia, eschscholzia, geranium, hemerocallis and nepeta, are encouraged to grow into each other to create a colourful tapestry effect that looks good even in a small space.

Anatomy of a border

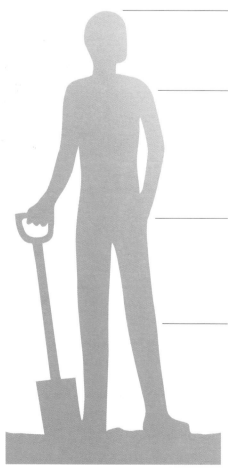

Shoulder high and above – trees
Choose standard trees that have a bare trunk to at least 1.2-1.5m (4-5ft), so that the crown is raised well up above smaller plants.

Waist to shoulder height – shrubs
Choose shrubs with a mixture of foliage colours (including variegated leaves), different flowering times and naturally tidy shapes that will slot in under trees. A sprinkling of evergreens provide winter interest. Shrubs that tolerate light shade are best for planting right underneath trees.

Knee to waist high – herbaceous flowers
Choose kinds that are happy to grow in light shade, because at various times of day they will be in dappled shade cast by bigger plants. In practice, this means all but the real sunlovers.

Ankle to knee high – annuals and carpeting plants
Choose plants that naturally sprawl or make low compact mounds to fill gaps in the bottom floor of the border between other plants. Alternatively, grow masses of spring bulbs to give the same effect early in the year before perennials have grown up again. Formal borders often have a row of identical edging plants, usually annuals, all round the front to give the bed a 'trim'.

Grandpa's Tip

Arrange the plants so that you can see them all properly.
● In a traditional border, plant taller plants at the back, with the very tallest centre-back. In front of them put successively shorter plants to create a tiered effect.
● In an island bed, plant the tallest plants in the centre, with concentric rings of shorter plants in front, so that the middle of the island is the highest point.

WHAT SHAPE OF BORDER?

Designer Tips

Some groups of plants stand out particularly well because they contain the right mixture of ingredients. The secret is to team together plants with contrasting shapes and textures, and choose colours that complement each other, rather than clashing.

• When planning a new border, cut pictures out of catalogues to see how plants look with various companions.

• If you spot striking groups of plants when visiting a garden, take a photo or make a note of the names so you can 'borrow' the idea to use at home.

• When buying plants in a nursery or garden centre, stand them together in groups to test the effect.

• At home, temporarily stand a new plant in place, still in its pot, to see how it looks with existing plants.

A traditional border

This runs round the edge of the garden, just in front of a wall, fence or hedge; it is usually quite wide. A formal border has a straight edge, an informal border has a curved one that looks much more natural. **ADVANTAGES** Traditional borders help to define the shape of the garden. With tall trees or shrubs around the edge of the garden, it is more sheltered and private. **DISADVANTAGES** They can be a lot of work, as weeds grow through from the garden next door, and plants get drawn up by lack of light at the back of the border. This means that you will need to stake many of the plants to keep them upright.

Island beds

These go in the middle of a lawn, where you can see them from all round. **ADVANTAGES** They are less work because plants grow shorter and stronger due to the better light. Only the tallest will need staking. The beds are easier to weed because you can get at them from all round. **DISADVANTAGES** They take up more room in a small garden, and can make mowing tricky.

Right: An island bed looks good with a centrepiece such as this Cedrus deodara. The conifer makes an all-year background for colourful seasonal flowers around the edges, such as the impatiens used here.

Narrow borders

These can run along either side of a path or along the edge of a feature such as a patio. Keep to smaller plants here, or the garden will start to look closed in and oppressive. **ADVANTAGES** They help to shape the garden and add colour and interest. **DISADVANTAGES** Too many small borders can make a garden look fussy and create a lot of extra work.

Left: Tropical beds are very showy, but most of the plants aren't hardy (such as the canna and dahlias shown here). This means that you will need somewhere to keep them safe from frost in winter when they are dormant.

Above: Herbaceous borders don't have to be too 'polite'. Tall plants growing in groups make a striking display against a brick wall or a backdrop of evergreen shrubs, which 'works' even if you don't have a huge garden.

Planting shrubs

Shrubs are woody-stemmed plants that create the basic shape of your garden, and are a good choice for a garden that is very easy to look after; once planted there is little to do, apart from routine weeding around them.

There are many different kinds of shrubs available, and you can choose them for particular 'looks' to suit any type of garden. Deciduous shrubs lose their leaves in winter, while evergreens keep theirs all year round. Some of the small compact shrubs make good plants for growing all year round in containers. You need some of each for seasonal colour and a leafy 'background'. Shrubs can vary in size from quite small plants suitable for a rock garden, such as hebes, to huge shrubs, such as *Viburnum rhytidophyllum*, that occupy as much room as a tree, so read the label before you buy.

Above: Most varieties of hebe grow naturally small and compact. They like sun and well-drained soil, so they are also good shrubs for tubs. The flowers are popular with bees.

MULTIPURPOSE SHRUBS

Where space is short, go for reliable, free-flowering plants, especially if they also have a second attraction at another time of year.

Chaenomeles (ornamental quince)
Good spring blossom. Medium-sized green fruits all summer ripen to gold in autumn.

Cornus alba 'Spaethii'
Green-and-gold variegated leaves and bright red stems, visible in winter after leaf fall.

Cotoneaster horizontalis
Herringbone-shaped fans of foliage that keep their tiny leaves in all but the worst winters. In autumn, the shape is outlined in small orange-red berries. Works equally well as ground cover or leaning up against a wall.

Fatsia japonica
Architectural-shaped evergreen with big 'fig-leaves'. Flowers in late autumn when there's not much happening in the garden, producing clusters of fluffy, cream-coloured balls.

Hamamelis (witch hazel)
One of the few good garden shrubs with brilliant autumn-tinted leaves. Spidery, scented, yellow, orange or red flowers appear on the bare stems in winter and early spring.

Pyracantha
Spiny evergreens that make a good intruder-proof boundary. Clusters of colourful berries last late into winter before being eaten by birds. Can be trained against a wall.

Above: Pyracantha grows into a big shrub, but if you want to keep it smaller, cut off the new shoots just beyond the clusters of flowers in midsummer. That way you'll also be able to see the berries better later.

Left: Fatsia is a favourite with flower arrangers, who cut single leaves or whole stems to use with cut flowers in a vase.

Below: Witch hazel (this is Hamamelis x intermedia 'Pallida') can grow quite big – up to 4.5m (15ft) in time – but can be pruned to keep it smaller. It's worth its space for the long-lasting autumn and winter colour.

GROWING SHRUBS IN TUBS

Choose naturally slow-growing, compact varieties. The tub will keep them even slower and smaller than usual by confining their roots. Evergreens are best for all-year-round effect, but some deciduous plants, such as Japanese maple, work well if they have a good shape that creates winter character.

If your soil isn't naturally acid, tubs are the best way to grow plants that need lime-free soil, such as rhododendrons and camellias, but choose the smaller varieties.

Plant in spring, using a 38-45cm (15-18in)-diameter container and soil-based potting mixture with some slow-release plant food granules mixed in. Choose ericaceous potting mixture for lime-hating plants, such as rhododendrons and camellias; these are usually peat-based, but soil-based versions are available now and last longer.

Water shrubs in tubs regularly all spring and summer, and protect them from waterlogging and freezing in winter (see page 41). Each spring, take off the top 2.5-5cm (1-2in) of potting mixture and replace it as shown below. Water lime-hating plants each spring with diluted sequestered iron, which acts as a tonic and helps prevent the leaves from turning yellow.

Above: *If you only want a shrub in a tub temporarily, there is no need to plant it properly. Simply stand it inside, still in its nursery pot. Add extra insulation in winter by lining the tub inside with bubblewrap.*

GOOD TUB SHRUBS
Bamboo
Camellia (lime-hater)
Hebe franciscana 'Variegata'
Cut-leaved Japanese maple
(*Acer palmatum* 'Dissectum' – prefers lime-free potting mix)
Dwarf rhododendron
(lime-hater)
Hardy yucca (*Yucca filamentosa* 'Variegata')

Topdressing a plant in a container

1 *Instead of repotting a shrub every year, topdress it instead. Scoop off the top 2.5-5cm (1-2in) of old potting mix and discard it. Topdressing is a way of 'freshening up' the mixture without the bother of repotting.*

2 *Combine some new potting mixture with a helping of slow-release feed granules (see maker's instructions). Top up the container to just below the rim to leave enough room for watering.*

3 *A standard-trained shrub in a tub looks impressive beside a front door, or you can use it to fill a temporary gap in a border. The standard pictured here is Euonymus japonicus 'Aureus'.*

Low-maintenance shrubs

For a glamorous garden that does not need much work, fill it with easy-care shrubs that don't need regular pruning. Evergreens are specially good for all-year-round effect, but also use plenty of deciduous kinds with varied flowering times to keep the garden changing through the seasons. Shrubs with good flowers and attractive foliage are doubly valuable in a small garden, as they provide two sets of interest in the same space.

Left: Tree peonies grow slowly and stay as medium-sized shrubs for many years. They need no pruning at all. The one shown here is Paeonia suffruticosa *'Souvenir de Maxime Cornu'. Tree peonies need a sheltered spot, otherwise the big flowers are spoilt by wind.*

Right: Weigela *'Florida Variegata' grows to about 90x90cm (36x36in) and makes a good plant to grow between roses, as the variegated leaves contrast well with them. The stems can also be cut and used for flower arranging.*

GREAT SHRUBS FOR LABOUR-SAVING GARDENS

Where time and space are short, go for naturally compact shrubs that are also very attractive and don't need pruning.

Hebe Compact evergreens with pretty 'bottlebrush' flowers all summer and often well into autumn.

Hardy hibiscus (*Hibiscus syriacus*) Slow-growing, upright shrubs with large flowers, similar to the houseplant.

Tree peony Huge tissue-papery flowers on compact deciduous shrub. Good foliage even when not flowering.

Hardy plumbago (*Ceratostigma willmottianum*) Dwarf shrubs with blue starry flowers in summer and autumn, plus autumn-tinted leaves.

Rosa 'Nozomi' When grown on a short stem, it makes a pile of weeping stems like a floral waterfall in summer.

***Weigela* 'Florida Variegata'** Small, compact shrub with cream-green variegated leaves and clusters of pink flowers in summer.

***Weigela florida* 'Foliis Purpureis'** Similar plant, but with plum-purple leaves and deeper pink flowers. Both lose their leaves in winter.

Right: For a container, raised bed or at the front of a border, the hardy plumbago (Ceratostigma willmottianum) is unbeatable. It dies down in winter in all but mild areas, but regrows the following spring.

Below: If the weather stays fine, hardy hibiscus will flower continuously from midsummer into autumn. The plants are neat and upright and don't need any pruning. This is Hibiscus syriacus 'Mauve Queen'.

Above: *Ornamental quince (Chaenomeles japonica) is a slightly untidy shrub, and a good choice for natural or cottage-style gardens. The large spring flowers are followed by plum-sized fruits that slowly ripen to golden orange in autumn. These persist late into the winter, so there's always something to look at. This one is 'Knap Hill Scarlet'.*

Below: *The herringbone cotoneaster (Cotoneaster horizontalis) makes pretty fans of foliage on stems lined with flowers in early summer and studded with orange-red berries in autumn. Grow it as ground cover or up against a low wall; it doesn't need any support or tying up.*

Grandpa's Tip

Low-maintenance gardens can often look the same all year round – boring. But by choosing a mixture of colourful flowering shrubs and attractive evergreens, then planting carpets of flowers underneath, including spring bulbs, such as *Anemone blanda*, and low perennials that don't mind light shade, such as lady's mantle (*Alchemilla mollis*), bergenia, hardy cranesbills, lamium and ajuga, you can make yourself a pretty garden and still see the changing seasons without having to do a lot of work.

Making the most of trees

Trees are ideal for providing height for the 'back row' of a mixed border, and a single specimen with plenty of character is perfect for planting in a lawn. These days, the average garden is comparatively small and there's not much room for trees, so it's worth choosing carefully. There are plenty of very attractive decorative kinds that won't outgrow their welcome, but if you only have room for one, make it a good one!

A specimen tree as a focal point

If you have a single tree growing in grass, make more of it by planting spring- and autumn-flowering bulbs in the grass underneath. For a slightly different effect in a wilder garden, make an informal area of bark chippings surrounded by logs. Suitable bulbs include dwarf daffodils, hardy cyclamen, snowdrops, scilla, chionodoxa, autumn crocus and colchicums.

GOOD 'CHARACTER' TREES FOR SMALL GARDENS

Acer pseudoplatanus 'Brilliantissimum' Very slow-growing 3m (10ft) tree with bright bronzy salmon-pink maple leaves.

Betula albosinensis (Chinese red birch) Typical birch, but with spectacular pinky red peeling bark. Eventually 6m (20ft).

Cercis siliquastrum (Judas tree) Naturally craggy, with kidney-shaped leaves and pink 'pea' flowers growing straight out of bare branches in late spring. Reaches 4.5m (15ft). Not suitable for cold regions.

Crab apple Many good varieties, such as 'John Downie' and 'Red Jade', with large spring blossom followed by small berrylike or larger rosehip-shaped fruit that attracts birds in autumn. Well-shaped trees that look good in winter.

Gleditsia triacanthos 'Rubylace' Attractive tree, eventually reaches 4.5m (15ft), with delicate ferny foliage that is red in spring, turning bronze later.

Salix caprea 'Pendula' (Kilmarnock willow) Small, well-behaved weeping tree with pussy willows in spring. Grows 1.8-3m (6-10ft), depending on the height of stem it has been grafted onto.

Right: Acer pseudoplatanus 'Brilliantissimum' is ideal for a small garden. This very slow-growing relative of the sycamore eventually reaches about 3m (10ft) tall, with pinky bronze foliage in spring.

Below: Clematis montana *can reach 6m (20ft), but when grown through a tree it simply covers the branches in early summer flowers and needs no pruning.*

Two for the space of one

If you already have a rather unexciting tree in the garden that you would rather improve than remove, consider growing a climber through it. Prepare a large planting hole about 1m (3ft) away from the base of the trunk, depending on the size of the tree, and dig in plenty of compost and some fertiliser. Plant the climber and train it up into the branches along a sloping pole. Clematis are the best kinds to grow this way as they don't smother the tree. There's no need to prune a clematis even if it is a variety that normally needs pruning. Just let it grow naturally, as this is the way they grow wild. If it's a big tree, plant two or three clematis, each with a different flowering time, and really bring your old tree to life.

Above: The spectacular Judas tree needs a mild garden. Masses of mauve-pink 'pea' flowers grow out of bare branches in early summer, followed by big, heart-shaped leaves.

Designer Tips

If other people's trees are overhanging your garden and making it shady, don't try to fight it. Where the soil is so full of tree roots that you can't dig it, spread garden compost over the area up to 10cm (4in) deep. Then plant spring bulbs, which do most of their growing before deciduous trees grow their leaves, and other things that don't mind dry shade. Try *Mahonia aquifolium*, *Iris foetidissima*, *Euphorbia robbiae*, ajuga, *Alchemilla mollis*, berberis, bergenia, *Lonicera pileata*, symphoricarpos (snowberry), vinca (periwinkle) and *Cotoneaster horizontalis*. Keep them watered until they become established, then mulch each spring with chipped bark to help retain moisture. For a more contemporary look, create a fantasy garden out of trained box shapes, make a 'land art' dragon or reptile out of old roofing tiles or rows of terracotta pots, or choose a natural look with logs and a seat.

Above: Growing a carpet of early dwarf bulbs under a tree adds an extra season of interest, and looks especially good against a craggy birch trunk. These are hardy Cyclamen coum.

Garden Doctor – Tree care

- Check variegated trees once or twice each summer and remove any all-green shoots. They grow faster than the patterned leaves and would eventually take over the plant.

- Cut off any sideshoots on the trunks of young trees to leave a clean trunk up to the level of the bottom branches.

- Don't grow grass right up to the trunk of a tree. You risk damaging the bark when mowing or using a rotary line trimmer. The latter can kill trees if they cut through a complete circle of bark round the trunk.

- Protect newly planted trees from rabbits, as these will strip the bark in winter. Surround the stems with a special spiral tree guard, which has holes punched in it for ventilation, or make a collar of wire netting at least 90cm (3ft) high.

- If you have a big tree in the garden that blocks out the light, don't try to do anything with it yourself – it's a job for a tree surgeon. He'll be able to lift the crown by removing the lowest branches, or thin it out to let more light through, without spoiling the shape of the tree.

Above: Rabbits can kill young trees by gnawing off the bark, so protect the bottom 90-120cm (36-48in) with a rabbit guard.

Left: When you buy a young tree, cut away any sideshoots from the bottom 90-120cm (36-48in) of the stem to help it form a bushy head at the top of a strong bare trunk, otherwise it tends to turn into a bush!

Growing perennials

Perennials are flowers that die down in autumn and spend winter as underground roots, but reappear each spring. They were traditionally used to make herbaceous borders, but nowadays they are very fashionable for growing in stylish borders and even containers all round the garden.

PERENNIALS FOR SUN

Hot, dry places make good gravel or seaside-style gardens, planted with sunloving, drought-tolerant perennials. If the soil is really poor, improve it by first digging in organic matter, then mulch with gravel to help retain moisture. Good perennials for this situation include:

Acanthus
Achillea
Alstroemeria
Artemisia
Crocosmia
Dianthus
Echinops ritro
Eryngium (sea holly)
Euphorbia wulfenii
Kniphofia
Lavender
Penstemon
Sedum spectabile
Sisyrinchium
Stachys

A year in the life of a perennial

Spring: New shoots start to appear through the soil. Weed, feed and mulch.
Late spring/early summer: Foliage grows up. Put frames or twigs into position to support tall plants.
Summer: Most perennial plants are in flower now. Deadhead regularly to encourage further flowers.
Autumn: Foliage slowly starts to turn yellow. Cut back to soil level, leaving the roots dormant underground for the winter.

Above: Give naturally floppy plants, such as this catananche, a support frame to grow through. Position it over the plants in spring, when the first shoots appear through the soil. Most of the frame will be hidden by leaves.

Right: Kniphofia 'Little Elf'. Red hot poker is a well-known summer flower that thrives in a hot dry spot. Many varieties have evergreen leaves, so don't cut them back in autumn; just tidy up dead leaves.

Achillea (this one is 'Coronation Gold') has flat-topped clusters of flowers all summer. These contrast well with 'spike-shaped' perennials.

Achillea 'Smiling Queen'

Crocosmia, once called montbretia, have lance-shaped leaves and flower all summer. Give them a sunny, well-drained spot and don't cut back the dead leaves until spring, as the underground corms like a little winter protection. This is Crocosmia 'Star of the East'.

DIVIDING PERENNIALS

Perennials need dividing when you can see the middle of the clump dying out, or if they stop growing or flowering well. Fast-growing kinds, such as Michaelmas daisies, may need dividing every three years, but slow ones, such as hostas, bergenia and lady's mantle (*Alchemilla mollis*), may not need attention until they have been growing for five years or more. Don't divide them until you need to!

Divide tough, vigorous perennials, such as Michaelmas daisies, in autumn, but leave slower or fleshy types, such as hostas, until spring, when they have just started to grow again and you can see small shoots.

Dig up the entire clump with as much root as possible. Lay it down on a firm surface such as a path, and cut through it with a sharp spade. Divide the plant into several pieces no smaller than about 10cm (4in) square. Throw away the unproductive old pieces from the middle of the clump and replant the best of the young divisions from around the edge.

In a small border, one piece will probably be enough, but in a bigger area, plant three pieces in a group about 20cm (8in) apart, which will quickly make more impact. You can plant the divisions back into the same place, but first improve the soil by digging in half a bucket of well-rotted compost and a sprinkling of general fertiliser.

Above: Michaelmas daisies such as this are easy to divide. Cut the old stems down, dig up the clump and simply chop it into several pieces with a sharp spade.

Right: Hellebores are invaluable for a small garden. Not only are they evergreen, but they also flower in spring, long before the majority of popular perennials. This is Helleborus x ericsmithii.

EVERGREEN PERENNIALS

A few perennials are evergreen, so they stay green instead of dying down in winter. They are used around the garden in the same way as 'proper' perennials, but they are specially valuable in small gardens or key places that are constantly on show, because they don't leave the borders looking bare in winter. They are worth looking out for; you'll find them on sale alongside other perennials at the garden centre.

Bergenia
Carex
Dianthus (pinks)
Euphorbia robbiae; E. wulfenii
Hellebores
Heuchera
Iris foetidissima
Liriope muscari (lily turf)
Many ornamental grasses

Grandpa's Tip

Peonies and bearded irises won't flower if you plant them too deep. Plant peonies so that the crowns are barely below the ground and no more than 2.5cm (1in) deep at the most. Plant bearded irises with the top half of each tuber above the ground, and in a spot where the sun is on them all day, or again they won't flower.

Below: Bergenia 'Silberlicht'. Bergenia is an easy-to-grow-anywhere perennial with superb 'elephant's ear'-shaped leaves and late spring flowers. The leaves of some varieties turn attractive shades of red or purple in winter.

Perennials with a purpose

Perennials are a varied group of plants and there are some to suit all sorts of situations around the garden, from hot and sunny to damp and shady. Naturally compact kinds with a long season of interest also make good plants for growing long term in containers.

BOG GARDEN PERENNIALS

The way to turn a problem wet spot into an attractive bed is to plant naturally damp-loving plants. Most also grow well in normal borders that never dry out badly. When preparing the ground for moisture-loving plants, dig in plenty of well-rotted organic matter so that it holds plenty of water, and mulch generously each spring.

Astilbe
Caltha palustris
Gunnera
Hardy ferns
Hosta
Ligularia
Lysimachia nummularia
Lythrum
Monarda
Polygonum
Primula
Rodgersia

Below: Astilbe are classic plants for damp to boggy soil, and also team well with candelabra primulas and hostas in light shade. This variety is Astilbe x arendsi 'Weiss Gloria', but there are also plenty of pink, red and magenta shades to choose from.

Above: Candelabra primulas, such as this Primula pulverulenta Bartley hybrid, have striking 'tiered' flowers in early summer. They look good growing with hostas, and both enjoy damp soil and light shade.

Right Caltha palustris 'Flore Pleno' is the double form of marsh marigold. It is equally at home in a bog garden, shallow water at the edge of a pond, or in a container standing in a large saucer of water.

Left: Cultivated forms of the wild purple loosestrife are more compact and colourful, but won't spread and take over. This variety is Lythrum salicaria 'Feuerkerze'.

PERENNIALS FOR CONTAINERS

If you don't want the bother of replanting annuals every season, why not consider growing perennials instead? Choose compact kinds with a long flowering season or good foliage. Good container perennials include:

Ajuga
Dwarf alstroemeria
Hostas
Houttuynia 'Chameleon'
Evergreen grasses and sedges, including *Festuca glauca, Carex comans* and *Carex* 'Evergold'

Plant in late spring, using a strong, frost-proof container and a soil-based potting mixture to which you have added some slow-release plant food. Water regularly from mid-spring to early autumn. When deciduous kinds turn yellow in autumn, cut them down 2.5cm (1in) above the top of the potting mix. In winter, keep containers of perennials outdoors, but raise the tubs on bricks to increase drainage and prevent waterlogging. If they are close to a wall, check every two weeks in case they get dry. In prolonged cold spells, move the tubs under cover or insulate them with bubblewrap to prevent the potting mixture freezing solid, which could kill the plant or break the pot. Each spring, scrape the top 2.5-5cm (1-2in) of old potting mixture out of the tub, replace it with a fresh supply and add some more slow-release plant food.

Above: Most grasses make good plants for containers. This is Hakonechloa macra 'Alboaurea', which dies down in winter, but evergreen kinds are good all year round. Don't cut them back.

Left: Hostas and hardy ferns are both brilliant in pots and ideal for a shady spot where bedding plants won't be happy. The best way to grow hostas in a slug-prone garden is to smear plant-protecting jelly around the pots to make a complete barrier.

Growing herbs

Herbs are handy in the kitchen and fashionable in the garden, and those with attractive scent are doubly welcome. There is no need to make a separate herb garden; herbs can be grown in flower beds, in the vegetable garden, or in a pretty 'potager'. Where space is short, most of the popular kinds make good plants for containers. If you cut lightly, you can still use them for cooking or to preserve for winter use.

MEDITERRANEAN HERBS

Bay, oregano, rosemary, sage and thyme. All these reasonably hardy sunlovers need very well-drained, not-too-fertile soil and a warm, sheltered, sunny spot. All but oregano are evergreen, and all grow into small, compact shrubs, except bay, which eventually makes a tree. It is often grown in a pot and trained into a small standard or pyramid shape. Taking cuttings is easy – see page 43.

Below: Purple sage (here with thyme) is as good for cooking as the plain green variety.

How to grow herbs in containers

Use a large container – a terracotta or glazed ceramic pot looks good planted with herbs. Place a layer of bits of broken clay pot or a handful of coarse gravel or pebbles in the bottom for drainage, and half-fill the container with soil-based potting mixture. Stand the plants inside, still in their pots, while you decide how you want to arrange them. Then take the herbs out of their pots, stand the rootballs in place and fill the gaps with more mixture. Water well. Soil-based potting mixture contains enough nutrients so that you won't need to give any extra feed for three months. After that, the easiest way to feed is to push a slow-release feed pellet or stick into the middle of the pot. Then, each time you water, a steady supply of plant food is automatically released.

Above: A planter like this contains enough herbs for culinary use. Pot up in spring or early summer and cut regularly to keep the herbs tidy. Replace annual herbs each spring and replant perennial evergreen kinds out in the garden.

OTHER POPULAR PERENNIAL HERBS

Chives, mint, tarragon and fennel. These are larger plants that can spread – in the case of mint, by runners. Tarragon and chives make clumps that slowly spread, and both chives and fennel self-seed freely. They need moist, fertile soil and sun for at least half the day. They are all hardy.

DECORATIVE AS WELL AS USEFUL HERBS

Borage, chamomile, lemon verbena, lavender, pinks and scented-leaved pelargoniums. These are prettier than they are genuinely useful – most people only use small amounts – so add one or two to containers to 'pretty up' the greener, culinary herbs. Add them to flower borders or plant them for fragrance close by places where you sit.

All those listed need similar conditions to Mediterranean herbs, except borage, which is an annual. Lemon verbena and scented-leaved pelargoniums are not hardy, so you will need to bring them indoors for the winter. If you don't have room for the old plants, root cuttings in small pots in late summer and keep these on a windowsill indoors for the winter instead.

Below: The blue starry flowers of borage are edible and can be used to decorate salads or buffet tables. Freeze them into ice cubes to liven up summer drinks.

ANNUAL HERBS

Basil, chervil, dill, parsley and pot marjoram. Grow them in moist, fertile soil, where they get sun for at least half the day. Some annual herbs, such as basil and chervil, quickly run to seed, so with these you need to sow several crops each year.

The curled form of parsley is the most popular for garnishes.

PROPAGATING HERBS

Growing evergreen herbs from cuttings

Cut about 7.5cm (3in)-long shoots from the tips of young stems any time during the summer, strip off the leaves from the bottom half of the stem (see below) and push several cuttings into a pot of soil-based seed mix, about 2.5cm (1in) apart. Water well, and cover the pot with a loose plastic bag. Stand it on a windowsill indoors out of the sun, and most will have rooted in about eight weeks. (Bay takes a lot longer.) When they are rooted, pot each cutting in separate pots and pinch out the growing tips to make them grow bushier. Use this method for evergreen herbs, plus lavender, lemon verbena and scented-leaved pelargoniums.

Growing annual herbs from seed

The best way to raise herbs from seed is by sowing seeds thinly in pots on a warm windowsill indoors in spring. This way they germinate rapidly. Instead of pricking out each seedling individually, wait until they are 2.5cm (1in) high and then tip them out, divide them up into three to five clumps and pot complete clumps. This gives you much bushier plants straightaway. When they are big enough, harden them off and plant herbs in containers or out in the garden. Keep the spares in pots on the kitchen windowsill to use in cooking while you are waiting for the rest to grow. And don't put frost-tender herbs, such as basil, outside until a week or more after the last frost.

Dividing perennial herbs

You can propagate herbs that die down in winter, such as mint, chives and oregano, by digging up clumps in spring and dividing them like perennial flowers. You can usually pull herbs apart with your fingers. Replant the pieces in the garden or in pots.

Below: Divide chives by tearing the ball of roots in two. First shake off as much soil as you can so you can see what you are doing.

Taking rosemary cuttings

1 *Gently remove the leaves from the bottom half of a healthy, non-flowering rosemary shoot, taking care not to 'peel' the stem.*

Prepare three cuttings, since they probably won't all 'take'.

2 *Push in the cuttings around the sides of a 9cm (3.5in) pot filled with seed mixture. Stand them on a windowsill out of bright sun.*

3 *Water in the cuttings, but then only water to stop the mix from drying out. If it's kept too damp, the cuttings will rot. Once rooted, pot each cutting separately.*

Grandpa's Tip

To stop mint spreading, grow it in a leaky bucket or a big flowerpot and sink that almost to its rim in the garden. Plant mint in soil-based potting mixture, but don't fill the bucket quite to the top. Leave a 5cm (2in) gap, so that there is a low barrier that stops the mint runners getting out and escaping into the garden. Mint is a greedy plant, so it needs repotting into fresh potting mixture every spring, otherwise it fades away. And apply liquid feed generously.

Growing bulbs

To make the most of a small garden, it is essential to pack in as many plants as possible. Bulbs are specially valuable, as they pop up, flower and then duck underground again. Plant bulbs as the bottom layer of a tiered planting scheme, under shrubs and perennials, so there is always something new coming out in bloom to keep the garden changing throughout the seasons.

Above: Daffodils are the traditional 'first sign of spring', but choose dwarf varieties if you don't like the sight of long floppy foliage for weeks after the flowers are over (see page 45 for tips on bulb care after flowering).

Planting in containers

Plant spring-flowering bulbs in autumn and summer-flowering bulbs in spring. If the container is a large one, stand it where you want the bulbs to flower; once filled it will be very heavy to move. Good places include the patio or the front doorstep. Put some drainage material in the bottom of the pot and cover this with 2.5cm (1in) of soil-based potting mixture.

Put in as many bulbs as you can, but do not let them quite touch each other or the sides of the pot. Press them firmly down. Cover the bulbs with 2.5cm (1in) of potting mix. Repeat with a second layer of bulbs. If the container is deep enough, add a third layer. It won't matter if the tips of the bulbs end up showing above the surface of the mix after the container has been filled. If the bulbs don't come quite to the top of the mix, plant the top of the container thickly with annuals so there is something to look at before the bulbs start to flower. Water just enough to dampen the potting mixture evenly and check it regularly; don't overwater but don't let the mix dry out, either.

1 *Dwarf gladioli make a good show in patio pots for the summer. Plant the corms 3.75cm (1.5in) apart in spring and cover them with 2.5cm (1in) of potting mixture.*

2 *The spear-shaped foliage makes a good foil for pots of bedding plants before the spikes of colourful trumpet-shaped flowers appear in midsummer. Gladioli die down in autumn, but the same corms flower again the following year.*

Above: Growing bulbs in containers, such as these 'Angelique' tulips, not only creates attractive displays, but also gives you the opportunity to move them around the garden.

Scientific Stuff

Gardeners tend to call any plant with an underground storage organ a 'bulb', even when technically it may be a tuber, corm or rhizome. You will find all these types of plant sold as dry 'bulbs' in the same section of the garden centre, and by post in bulb catalogues.

The embryo daffodil encased in scales

Base plate and roots

A true bulb (e.g. daffodil) is a series of scales attached to a base plate at the bottom of the bulb. A corm (such as crocus) is really a short stem that replaces itself annually. A tuber (such as dahlia) is a swollen stem or root, e.g. potato, adapted for storage. A rhizome (e.g. lily-of-the-valley) is a stem that creeps beneath ground level.

SUMMER AND AUTUMN BULBS

A YEAR IN THE LIFE OF A SPRING BULB

Autumn Planting time.
Winter The bulb takes root and in late winter shoots appear above the ground.
Spring Flowering time. Most of the bulb's energy reserves are used up in producing leaves and flowers, and it shrinks.
Late spring As the flowers finish, the leaves are using sunlight to make carbohydrates that refill the bulb.
Early summer Six to eight weeks after flowering, leaves start turning yellow, the bulb is stocked with winter stores and contains a tiny 'bud' that will produce the following year's flowers.
Summer until autumn The bulb is dormant underground, safe from predators and drought.

Grandpa's Tip

Don't cut down the foliage of spring bulbs until at least six weeks after they finish flowering, or they won't flower next year. For the same reason, don't mow grass where bulbs are naturalised during this time. And don't knot your daffodil foliage either; it doesn't look very nice and it stops the leaves doing their job properly.

Planting bulbs in beds and borders

As a good rule of thumb, plant bulbs to three times their own depth. Exceptions are *Lilium candidum*, where the tip of each bulb should show just above the ground, and hardy cyclamen – the tops of their tubers should be just above ground.

To make bulbs look as if they grew naturally, drop a handful on the ground and plant them where they fall.

Use a trowel or bulb planter to make a hole for each bulb and press the bulb firmly down into the bottom. Then replace the plug of soil that you removed when making the hole and cover the bulb with it.

SUMMER AND AUTUMN BULBS

Summer bulbs

'Summer bulbs' covers a wide range of hardy and non-hardy plants.
Hardy plants: Lilies can be planted in spring or autumn, depending on when bulbs are available, but do not leave them out of the ground for long, as they dislike drying out. Once planted, they are best left undisturbed to build up slowly into bigger clumps.
Non-hardy plants: Plant canna and tuberous begonia in pots in a heated greenhouse and don't move them outdoors until

Above: Spectacular red cannas are perfect for adding a tropical touch to summer borders. Bring them inside for the winter.

after the last frost. Dahlia tubers are usually planted dry in late spring, but because they are planted 7.5cm (3in) deep, there is no risk of the tender shoots appearing above

Above: When planting bulbs in grass, punch out a neat hole using a proper bulb planter. To release the 'core' of soil it removes, loosen your grip on the handle.

Above: Autumn-flowering colchicum bulbs are expensive, but each one produces several flowers and spreads slowly. This variety is Colchicum bivonae syn. bowlesianum.

the ground when a frost might nip them off. Tigridia and acidanthera bulbs are planted in the garden around the time of the last frost. Frost-tender bulbs must be harvested in autumn before the first frost. Dry off the bulbs and store them in a frost-free place until the next planting time comes round.

Autumn bulbs

Autumn crocus and colchicums are only available for a few weeks in late summer. Plant them straightaway, as they flower within a few weeks. Once in the ground they can be left alone and will slowly increase naturally, building up colonies.

Bulb care

To stop squirrels stealing your flower bulbs, bury a piece of small-mesh chicken wire 2.5cm (1in) below the surface over the area where the bulbs are growing. This also stops you slicing into dormant bulbs when you are hoeing.

If soil pests are a problem, dust bulbs with pesticide powder before planting. If mice are your problem, plant bulbs with a layer of holly leaves over the top. They take several years to rot.

To avoid new bulbs rotting in damp soil, sit them onto 2.5cm (1in) of grit in the bottom of their planting holes and sprinkle them with yellow sulphur dust.

Plant late-rooting bulbs, such as tulips and hyacinths, in mid- to late autumn, two months after early-rooting ones such as daffodils. Ideally, plant these as soon as they appear in the shops. Contrary to what the old gardening books say, there's no need to deadhead bulbs.

Growing roses

Roses are the most popular garden plants ever, found in nearly 90% of gardens. There are several different groups of roses, each with their own flowering seasons and size that make them best for particular situations. You no longer need to plant formal rose beds – modern compact kinds can be used like any flowering shrub, and even planted in containers.

Above: Patio roses, such as this 'Sweet Dreams', need a rich, soil-based potting mixture and regular feeding with liquid tomato feed when grown in containers. Choose a 30-38cm (12-15in)-diameter pot.

Left: Rosa mundi *is an old-fashioned rose dating back to about the fourteenth century, but still popular for its stripy flowers. It is a small, bushy plant, about 90x90cm (36x36in), with a short flowering season in early summer.*

Anatomy of a rose

Roses are actually two plants joined together, with the stems of one variety growing on the roots of another. For the gardener, grafted plants can create work, as the rootstock often sends up strong suckers that grow faster than the named variety. Unless dealt with, they can take over from the named variety. The stems of rootstocks are relatively thorn-free and their leaves often, but not always, have a different number of leaflets. Trace back a suspect stem. If it originates underground, it is almost certainly a sucker. Dig carefully round it with a trowel and find the point where it emerges from a root, then tear it out. If you cut suckers off at ground level, they grow back worse than ever. If you find it easier, you can spray suckers carefully with a paraquat-based weedkiller in spring when they are soft and first push through the soil, but protect surrounding plants.

Named variety

Rootstock

Graft union, which often looks like a bulge at the base of the plant.

ROSE TERMS

Named variety is the cultivated rose with large, spectacular flowers.

The rootstock is a form of wild rose, specially grown for this purpose. The flowers are 'wild-looking', and rootstocks often have rosehips.

Suckers are strong shoots growing directly from the roots of the rootstock. They often grow more vigorously if the plant has been dug up and moved, or when the roots have been damaged with a hoe when weeding.

THE DIFFERENT TYPES OF ROSES

• **Modern bush roses** include the popular hybrid teas and floribundas that flower almost continuously from early summer to the first autumn frosts. Prune them hard each year in early spring, apply a rose food and mulch generously with well-rotted organic matter. They used to be grown in formal rose beds on their own, but nowadays they are often planted in mixed borders.

• **Patio roses** are very compact, free-flowering versions of bush roses and ideal for growing in tubs. Prune lightly in early spring to keep them in shape. Feed and mulch as described above.

• **Groundcover roses** are low-growing, spreading or semi-creeping kinds, good for covering sunny banks or the fronts of borders if they are free of perennial weeds; it is very difficult to weed through a carpet of prickly stems! Prune lightly to keep them in shape in early spring.

• **Miniature roses** are much more fragile. Although often sold in pots as houseplants, they are best grown outdoors in a sheltered, sunny spot, in rich but well-drained ground;

Below: Climbing and rambler roses are ideal for covering arches, pergolas or trellis with summer colour. Some varieties flower once, some twice-yearly, and some for much of the summer, so check when you buy.

they do well in raised beds and containers. No pruning is needed, but use scissors to remove dead shoots in late spring.

• **Shrub roses** are more closely related to the wild species, with simple flowers, often followed by large or colourful rosehips. They are ideal for more natural gardens and can make good prickly hedging, but they can also be grown in mixed borders. Regular pruning isn't needed; just tidy the shape in early spring if they need it.

• **Old-fashioned roses** are hybrids with long-lost pedigrees, often dating back a century or more. They have characteristic blowsy flowers or shallow, bowl-shaped heads divided into 'quarters', quite unlike modern roses. Some have exceptional perfume. Treat old-fashioned roses as if they were flowering shrubs and grow them in mixed borders or in cottage-style gardens, underplanted with a mixture of low, spreading perennials and spring bulbs. These provide colour and interest outside the rose's short flowering season, which only lasts for a few weeks in summer. Prune after flowering, removing the dead flowers, plus 15cm (6in) of stem. Thin out a few old overcrowded branches in winter.

• **Climbing roses** look very much like ordinary bush roses, except that instead of being bushy, they have a permanent framework of thick stems tied up to a wall or structure. Very little pruning is normally needed; just remove dead flowerheads with a good length of stem tip in summer.

• **Rambler roses** have quite a different type of growth, more like blackberry 'canes'. Vigorous varieties need pruning quite hard in autumn. Cut back the stems that have flowered to the point where they join a strong, new, unflowered shoot. But non-vigorous varieties only need deadheading.

• **All roses** need deadheading regularly. Cut off the dead head with 5-10cm (2-4in) of stem. Apply more rose food and water well in. (There are more details on deadheading techniques on page 88.)

Grandpa's Tip

Standard roses are just bush roses grafted onto a tall stem to make them look like small flowering trees. When prostrate groundcover roses such as 'Nozomi' are grafted onto stems, they make delightful, small, weeping trees – superb plants for all-year-round containers or as the centrepiece of a small flower bed.

Don't prune standard roses hard, or you may find that all you have left is the stem of the rootstock. Just prune lightly in mid-spring to reshape the head of the plant.

Above: 'Ballerina' is a modern shrub rose that flowers all summer and is especially attractive grown as a standard (on a tall stem) above a carpet of low flowers such as nepeta.

Growing hardy annuals

Hardy annuals are charming 'old-fashioned' flowers that are now making quite a comeback. Unlike summer bedding plants (also known as half-hardy annuals), hardy annuals are surprisingly cold-tolerant, so you can grow your own plants without needing a greenhouse or any special equipment. Just sow the seeds in pots or seed trays in a porch or car port, or into the ground in the garden, and move the plants to where you want them to flower when they are big enough to handle easily. Although hardy annuals die off at the end of the season, they often drop seeds in the soil that grow in autumn or the following spring.

Right: Sweet peas are popular hardy annuals for cutting. For the earliest flowers, sow seeds in pots in a cold greenhouse in autumn and plant them out in spring.

Grandpa's Tip

Old cottage gardeners didn't have the time or money to go in for a lot of fancy gardening techniques, so their gardens were the 'take-care-of-itself' variety. You can create the same haphazard effect at home, anywhere you want a border that doesn't need much looking after, so long as it gets the sun for about half the day. Start by planting a selection of cottagey-looking perennials that don't need digging up and dividing, such as lady's mantle (*Alchemilla mollis*), gardener's garters grass (*Phalaris arundinacea* 'Picta' or the new broad white-striped 'Feesey'), astrantia and campanula. In the soil around them sow Iceland poppies, clarkia, viola and godetia. Some of the perennials will spread and some will self-seed. The annuals will also self-seed, so that by year two they all mingle together, cover the ground and flower without you having to do more than lift out the odd weed that doesn't get smothered naturally, and remove any stray seedlings that come up where you don't want them. Red nasturtiums, orange calendula marigolds and bronze-leaved fennel make a good flowering combination for an easy cottage garden effect.

Sowing seeds in rows in the ground

1 *To get good, strong plants, sow the seeds very thinly along a groove in the ground. Space large seeds 2.5-5cm (1-2in) apart, or take tiny pinches of small seeds and sprinkle them like salt along the row. Imagine each seed growing into a plant!*

If you want plenty of hardy annuals all round the garden, the quick and easy way to raise large quantities is to borrow a couple of rows in the vegetable garden or an empty flower bed and turn it into a temporary nursery.

Fork the soil over well – there is no need to add fertiliser. Scratch a long, straight, shallow groove with the tip of a cane and sprinkle the flower seed thinly along it. Barely cover the seed with a fine scattering of sieved soil, and water using a fine rose on a watering can.

When seedlings appear, wait until they are a manageable size and then thin them out so that they have more room to develop. Once they make bushy young plants 5-7.5cm (2-3in) high, dig them up carefully with a hand fork and replant them where you want them to grow.

2 *When the seedlings are about 2.5cm (1in) high, 'weed' out the smallest ones, leaving the strongest spaced 7.5-10cm (3-4in) apart. Keep them watered in dry weather. Once the plants are 5-7.5cm (2-3in) high, they are ready to be moved to their flowering positions.*

HARDY ANNUALS FOR FUSS-FREE CONTAINERS

Below: Create an old-fashioned cottage garden look by growing a mixture of randomly planted hardy annuals or allow them to come up naturally from seed shed by the previous year's flowers.

HARDY ANNUALS

Alyssum
Clarkia
Convolvulus (dwarf morning glory)
Cornflower
Godetia
Iberis (candytuft)
Larkspur
Lavatera (annual mallow)
Matthiola bicornis (night-scented stock)
Nasturtium
Nigella (love-in-a-mist)
Sunflower
Sweet pea

Hardy annuals are the simple solution if you want to grow summer flowers that you can just sow straight into containers and leave to come up without any pricking out or transplanting. Good choices include naturally compact bushy kinds, such as dwarf nasturtiums. However, given a rustic tripod or similar structure to climb on, self-clinging climbers, such as sweet peas and canary creeper (*Tropaeolum peregrinum*), are very successful sown in hanging baskets or large pots. Short varieties of sunflower are also fun for sowing into good-sized 15-20cm (6-8in)-diameter terracotta pots.

Stand the containers where you want the plants to flower to avoid moving heavy containers about. Hardy annuals don't like over-rich soil, so fill each container with a seed mixture. Nasturtiums are best sown into a mixture used to grow something else the previous summer. They need really quite poor soil, otherwise they just produce huge leaves and very few flowers. Space out large seeds, such as nasturtiums and sweet peas, 2.5-5cm (1-2in) apart, so they have room to grow. When the seedlings come up, carefully

Left: Now that dwarf varieties are available, sunflowers are becoming very popular as container plants. They are easy to grow; sow the seeds straight into the pot.

pull out the weakest ones, leaving the rest 10-15cm (4-6in) apart. In the case of pots of sunflowers, plant a cluster of three or four seeds in the centre of each pot and push them down into the mixture so they are barely covered. Water well when the seedlings come up, leave the strongest one and pull out the rest. Keep all young plants watered and begin feeding when they have been growing for four to six weeks, except in the case of nasturtiums.

Sow hardy annuals in early to mid-spring, and if you keep them regularly watered and deadheaded, you'll have plants in flower for most of the summer.

Above: Leave the large heads of sunflowers on the plant after the petals have fallen and you will get circles of tightly packed sunflower seeds that will attract wild birds to feed. Nowadays, you can buy tall, giant sunflowers, short, bushy kinds with plenty of flowers, or miniatures for pots, with red and bronze flowers, as well as the familiar yellow.

Left: Nasturtiums won't flower if they are grown in rich soil; instead you get huge leaves. They are a good choice for containers if you are apt to forget the feeding!

Right: Don't deadhead nigella (love-in-a-mist), as the huge seed pods are good for drying for flower arrangements.

Growing plants from plugs

When you only have a few containers or small beds to fill, instead of buying bedding plants in trays containing four dozen identical plants, most people now prefer to buy much smaller quantities. Although choice varieties are sold individually in pots ready for planting in early summer, many people opt to buy them as plugs – young plants growing in multipacks that look rather like egg boxes. You can buy 'plug plants' by mail order from catalogues issued in spring by the seed firms and other specialist plant raisers, and plugs are also available at most good garden centres.

Left: Scaevola aemula *'Blue Wonder' is a popular plug plant often used in containers and hanging baskets, although it can also be planted in borders. The flowers are fan-shaped, hence the common name of 'fairy fans'.*

Grandpa's Tip

You can't just put delicate patio plants straight outdoors into wind, rain and fluctuating temperatures, when all they've ever known are stable conditions in a greenhouse or indoors. You need to toughen them up first. Start 'hardening them off' two to three weeks before the date you expect the last frost in your area; other gardeners will know when that is. Stand the plants outside on sunny days and bring them in again at night. If you have a cold frame or cloches, you can stand the plants underneath and just lift off the top during the day, which saves a lot of moving plants around. After three weeks it should be safe to plant them out, but choose a spell of good weather. If it turns cold, windy or very wet, wait until the conditions improve. And if you happen to plant out a bit too soon and a cold night is forecast, then cover containers of tender plants with several layers of horticultural fleece. It only gives a few degrees of frost protection, but that can be enough to make the difference between life and death.

Left: Pelargoniums are old favourites, available in a wide range of colours as well as the traditional red. They make good plants for pots as they don't mind an occasional drying out! They are often available as young plants in spring, as well as plugs.

Right: Verbena has become very popular as a hanging basket 'filler' now that it is available cheaply as a plug plant. Use it for contrast between large flowers such as petunia. This attractive variety is 'Homestead Purple'.

Right: Surfinia petunias are firm container favourites. If regularly deadheaded, they flower constantly from early summer to autumn. The scented flowers almost hide the plants. This is 'Pink Vein'.

PICK OF THE PLUGS

Plug plants are usually small seedlings, but they are sometimes supplied as tiny rooted cuttings. It doesn't matter, as you treat them both the same way. Here are the very best varieties that will keep your containers looking colourful from the start of summer right through into autumn.

California Dreamers A range of fuchsia varieties with exceptionally large, flamboyant flowers, but they need a warm spot to really do well.

Continental cascading pelargoniums Special varieties of trailing ivy-leaved pelargoniums. They have flowers with narrow petals, but in such huge numbers as to smother the plants, which flower profusely all summer.

Diascia Spreading stunner, with short spikes of flower in coral or salmon-pink shades. Good in warm conditions, and with a very long flowering season.

Surfinia petunias Large, scented, weatherproof flowers on strong cascading plants. One of the best container plants; it keeps flowering vigorously right through the summer.

Million Bells petunias Smaller flowers, but masses more of them and even more weather-resistant.

Scaevola Masses of small, purple, fan-shaped flowers along rather stiff horizontal stems that make a good frill round the edge of a tub.

Trailing snapdragons Grey furry leaves form a mound of felt-studded white or pink flowers, picked out in lemon. Long flowering season.

Trailing verbena Pretty and free-flowering plants in a range of colours for a more traditional effect. Good with fuchsias.

Potting up mail-order plug plants

Bellis daisies

1 In order to travel safely by post, mail order plug plants are supplied with quite substantial packaging. It is vital to take them out of the pack as soon as possible after delivery, even if you don't have time to plant them straightaway.

2 If you don't have time to deal with the plants for now, stand the pack in a tray and moisten lightly by spraying them with tepid water. Keep them in a heated greenhouse or sunroom, or on a warm, well-lit windowsill indoors.

3 As soon as you have time, pot each plug plant individually into a 9cm (3.5in) pot filled with potting mixture. If you have many of one kind, you can push them into seedtrays, spacing them 5cm (2in) apart.

4 Don't push them in too far. The top of the plug of roots should be roughly level with the surface of the potting mixture surrounding them. If the mixture is soft, there's no need to make a hole, as the point at the tip of the plug of roots is specially designed to be pushed in.

5 Water thoroughly and return to a warm windowsill. When the plants are 5cm (2in) high 'stop' them (pinch the tops out) to make them grow bushy. After they have been growing for four to six weeks, begin watering with liquid tomato feed diluted to one quarter the normal strength. The plant food in the potting mixture will be almost used up by then.

Container gardening

Containers are 'go-anywhere' gardens that make it easy to grow plants wherever there is no soil, such as on paths and paving, but they are most popular for decorating patios. Although they are best-known for creating glamorous bedding plant displays in summer, containers can be kept looking colourful all the year round just by replanting them at the start of each new season. Alternatively, opt for low-maintenance schemes with year-round shrubs and evergreens that remain in the same containers for several years.

Scientific Stuff

If you want to grow lime-hating plants, such as rhododendrons, but your garden soil isn't suitable, grow them in pots of ericaceous mix. This is lime-free, so that the plants can get enough iron, which is 'locked up' by chalk.

SPRING BEDDING

Spring bulbs
Polyanthus
Coloured primroses
Ranunculus

TIP: As the plants don't have time to grow, plant spring bedding thickly, otherwise the container will always look half empty.

Below: Tulipa *'Black Parrot' and violas in an iron trough flowering in spring.*

Above: As an alternative to planting one large container, group together several smaller seasonal pots of plants.*

AUTUMN BEDDING

Ornamental cabbage
Winter-flowering pansies

TIP: Plant a couple of layers of spring bulbs, such as dwarf daffodils, under winter-flowering pansies to keep the same container looking good until late spring.

CLIMBERS FOR CONTAINERS

Annuals:
Black-eyed Susan (*Thunbergia alata*)
Morning glory (*Ipomoea*)
Sweet peas
All year round:
Clematis

TIP: Push a metal or rustic trellis obelisk into the container before planting. Don't try to add it afterwards or you'll break the plants.

GOOD ALL-YEAR-ROUND PLANTS FOR CONTAINERS

Box (trimmed as potted topiary)
Camellia
Cut-leaved Japanese maple
(*Acer palmatum* 'Dissectum')
Dwarf rhododendron
Evergreen grasses and sedges, such as festuca and carex

TIP: Each spring use an old tablespoon to remove the top 2.5cm (1in) of potting mix, then top up the container with fresh soil-based mix with some slow-release fertiliser added.

SUMMER BEDDING

Argyranthemum
Fuchsias
Pelargoniums
Petunias
Other annual bedding and patio plants

TIP: Mix water-retaining gel crystals into the potting mixture before planting to help keep plants moist when the weather gets hot.

Right: Plant frost-tender bedding plants in early summer. They will make a good display until autumn.*

WINTER BEDDING

Ivies
Euonymus
Winter-flowering heathers
Gaultheria procumbens
Skimmia reevesiana

TIP: Use small shrubs for winter colour and then replant them in the garden in spring.

Right: A container of *Pennisetum purpureum*, Carex *'Silver Sceptre'* and Heuchera *'Plum Pudding'*, make a frosty picture on a crisp winter morning.*

Garden Doctor – Potting mixture

- Don't economise by using garden soil to fill containers. When plants are confined in a crowded space, they cannot grow and flower well unless their roots are in good growing conditions.
- Soil-less potting mix is fine for shortlived plants, such as summer bedding, but choose a soil-based mixture for plants that will remain in containers for years on end, such as potted shrubs, as it 'lasts' longer.
- If soil pests have been a problem in the past, avoid them by using a potting mix containing pesticide. Various kinds are now available from garden centres.
- Refill tubs with fresh potting mixture each year before planting summer bedding. You can re-use what's left of the old mixture, topped up with some more from a new bag, when you replace the plants with autumn, winter or spring bedding.
- When you finally tip out containers, use the old mixture on the garden as a free soil improver.

Planting a tub

1 *This terracotta tub is porous, so line it with black plastic, making sure there is a drainage hole in the bottom.*

2 *Part-fill the container with potting mixture. Keeping the plants in their pots, arrange them roughly round the container, so you can see where they will look best.*

3 *Tip the plants gently out of their pots one by one and tuck them into position, then top up with more potting mix and water well.*

Grandpa's Tip

For winter use, you need sturdy containers that won't shatter if they happen to freeze; wood or plastic are best. If you choose terracotta or ceramics, insist on frostproof kinds, even though they cost a little more.

Winter containers suffer badly from waterlogging, so stand them in a sheltered spot, say, next to a wall. Raise them up on a couple of bricks or special pot feet to improve the drainage, so that they can't stand in a puddle.

If a long icy spell is forecast, insulate outdoor containers by tying newspapers or bubblewrap around them so that the compost won't freeze solid.

Container care

Watering Check containers daily in summer and once a week in winter. Water whenever the potting mixture starts to feel dry.

Feeding Use liquid or soluble feeds (not granular or solid types). Feed weekly from late spring until late summer. Alternatively, mix slow-release fertiliser granules into the potting mixture before planting a summer container. Do not feed containers in winter.

Deadheading To keep plants blooming right through the season, remove dead flowerheads regularly.

Hanging baskets

Hanging baskets are amongst the most spectacular of containers, but because they are open to the air on all sides, they dry out much faster than containers at ground level. For striking results, the right ingredients and regular attention are essential. If time is short, plant up one or two really big baskets instead of several small ones. You can replant them each season for year-round colour.

Which basket?

- The traditional hanging basket is made of a wire framework with open sides. It needs to be lined before it can hold any potting mix. Although a wire basket looks most attractive when lined with moss and with plants growing in both sides and top, the big drawback is that it dries out faster than any other kind of hanging basket and also drips badly, which can be a nuisance.
- Solid-sided plastic baskets may not initially look so attractive, because you can only plant the top and not the sides, and to start with, the plastic is very visible. But this type of basket is more practical for many

people as it doesn't dry out so fast or drip so much (some kinds include a drip tray). If planted with vigorous trailing varieties, the plastic is soon hidden by plants. A solid-sided basket does not need lining and is very quick to plant up.

- Self-watering baskets are similar to other solid-sided kinds, except that they have a water reservoir built into the base. This is enough to keep the potting mixture moist for up to two days, so these baskets need much less attention than usual.
- Rustic baskets are becoming popular. These are woven from willow or twigs and have a relatively short life, as the natural materials will eventually discolour and

Above: Here, a very free-form hanging basket display is combined with wall-pots of creeping Jenny and an actinidia climber to create a cottage garden-look.

rot due to contact with damp potting mix. Lining with a waterproof material such as black plastic extends their life, or else paint them with a coat of yacht varnish.

What liner?

- Rigid liners made of compressed fibre are available in various sizes to fit inside hanging baskets. They are quick and convenient to use, but when placed in a wire basket they prevent you from planting through the sides.
- Flexible liners are available in a range of materials, from natural hessian to plasticised materials. They consist of a circle of flaps that overlap like the petals of a flower when placed inside a hanging basket. Various sizes are available to fit different baskets. With these liners, you can plant through the sides of a wire basket, as you can push plants between the flaps.
- DIY liners can be made from all sorts of materials, including circles cut from woollen jumpers or strong black plastic. You can use an old potting mixture bag, which is black on the inside; make sure the black side faces outwards when placed in the basket.
- Moss. Don't gather moss from the woods; you can buy bags of moss specially for hanging baskets, or if you have moss in your lawn you can rake that out to use. Any moss will turn brown after a time, especially if it is allowed to dry out. Synthetic moss made of green-dyed stringy fibres is available in garden centres. It looks good and because it is very free-draining, it is particularly good for use in winter hanging baskets.

BEST PLANTS FOR SUMMER BASKETS

Brachyscome
Diascia
Continental cascading pelargoniums
Surfinia and Million Bells petunias
Sutera
Trailing fuchsias
Trailing lobelia
Trailing snapdragons
Trailing verbena

Right: Two contrasting flower shapes and sizes always 'work' well together, such as the trailing pelargoniums and brachyscome used here.

GOOD WINTER BASKET PLANTS

Ivies
Coloured primroses
Prostrate rosemary
Santolina
Creeping thyme

Left: Winter baskets of ivy, winter heather and ornamental cabbages look best hung low enough so that you can see into them.

Grandpa's Tip

When preparing a moss-lined wire basket for planting, cover the base with a layer of moss and place an old dish in the bottom. This internal water reservoir will help to prevent the basket from drying out so fast.

SECRETS OF SUCCESS

Mix up your own special hanging basket potting mixture. Take ordinary potting mixture, stir in water-retaining crystals and add water. Then add slow-release fertiliser granules. Use this mixture to fill the basket in the usual way.

Sprinkle the right quantity of dry crystals over the mix and stir well. Add water to rehydrate the gel.

When the gel has absorbed enough water and looks like rubbery sections of jelly, add slow-release fertiliser. Now the mixture is ready to use.

For show-winning results, start liquid feeding four to six weeks after planting, even if you used slow-release fertiliser in the potting mix. Use liquid tomato feed diluted to half the usual strength once or twice each week. Water plants well.

Planting up a hanging basket

Ingredients:
One 35.5cm (14in)-diameter wire-framed hanging basket
A bag of moss
Hanging basket potting mixture
A selection of trailing plants

1 *Line the base with moss and add 5cm (2in) of potting mix. Take five plants and push the roots through the holes so that the stems rest on the moss 'collar', forming a ring around the base. If the basket is unstable, support it in a bucket.*

2 *Build up the sides of the basket with another layer of moss about 5cm (2in) deep and top up with potting mixture. Add another layer of plants as before, placing them so they are not directly above the previous row. Position one taller plant in the middle.*

3 *Fill any gaps with petunias, so that the basket is completely packed with plants. This produces a basket that not only looks good straightaway, but also has the potential to grow into something really stunning.*

4 *Water thoroughly and hang in position. Since the basket is so full of plants, their roots will soon occupy all the space, and the basket will dry out very quickly. You may need to water twice daily.*

A raised salad bed

You don't need much room to grow salad leaves; they are so productive that a bed measuring 90x180cm (3x6ft) is enough to keep a family of salad-lovers going all summer. They are very little work, too. In a bed with raised sides, the soil is deeper than usual, which means that you can plant crops close together, but don't tread on the ground after it has been prepared.

Routine care

Feeding Before sowing, sprinkle blood, fish and bone fertiliser over the soil at the rate recommended and rake well in. To keep crops growing vigorously, apply diluted organic liquid feeds or liquid seaweed extract when they are roughly half grown.
Watering Keep the soil in a salad bed moist at all times, as salad crops are very shallow-rooted. If the soil dries out badly, leaf salads often bolt and lettuces may taste bitter.

Weeding Hoe carefully between rows until the plant leaves touch and cover the ground. Hoe very shallowly to avoid damaging roots.
Clearing As soon as a row of salad has been cut, clear up the leaves, weeds and debris, sprinkle fertiliser carefully over the bare soil (to avoid scorching, wash it off adjacent leaves if it blows onto them). Then lightly fork over the ground, rake it level and sow or plant the next crop straightaway.

Sowing seeds

1 *Prepare the soil (see page 25) and rake in some fertiliser. Then lay a plank over the soil to work from. Make a shallow groove along the edge of the plank with a trowel.*

2 *Sprinkle seeds thinly along the groove and cover them with soil. The seedlings will grow in a straight line, which makes weeding easier. Thin them out when they are big enough to handle.*

POPULAR SALAD CROPS

Lettuce Sow summer varieties from mid-spring to midsummer. Sow fast-maturing varieties in late summer to cover with cloches for autumn use. Winter lettuce are worth trying, but very much at the mercy of the weather and best grown under glass. Grow a few each of several different types of lettuce for a constant supply of varied, colourful and interesting salads.

Cabbage lettuce Traditional round green lettuce. Small varieties, such as 'Tom Thumb', are ideal for compact salad beds as you plant them closer together and so fit more into the space. Little waste.

Cos lettuce (romaine) Superb flavour, but tall varieties need tying round with raffia when half-grown to make them form hearts. Tricky to grow well; they often bolt in hot or dry weather. Semi-cos varieties, such as 'Little Gem', are easy to grow, don't need tying up and taste delicious.

Oak leaf lettuce Good flavour and pretty leaf shapes make them suitable for mixed leaf salads or as garnishes. You can usually pick a few leaves and leave the rest to grow.

Red lettuce Very decorative but not always the best-flavoured, so experiment until you find your favourite varieties.

Cut-and-come-again lettuce Varieties such as 'Salad Bowl' allow you to cut a few leaves at a time without harvesting the entire plant. You can do this for several months before the plant runs to seed.

Rocket Sow two to three times per year, from early spring to midsummer. Both the flowers and the leaves are edible.

Watercress Sow from spring to early summer or root thick old stems from the base of a bundle of watercress from the greengrocer in a glass of water and plant. Pick regularly to prevent flowering. Watercress grows well in any moist soil; a stream is not essential!

Land cress A good alternative to watercress but not so hot. Sow from early spring to midsummer.

Spring onions Sow thickly in spring and thin out the plants gradually. Use the plants you remove as spring onions at any stage, from baby to full-grown. This way, one row will last you all season.

Oriental leaves Sow a mixture of Chinese cabbage, pak choi, mizuma, etc., in early summer and cut as baby leaves. Or use thinnings in salads, leaving the remaining plants spaced 15-20cm (6-8in) apart to form hearts to use in autumn.

Baby spinach leaves Sow little and often, from early spring under cloches to late spring, then again in late summer for an autumn crop. In summer, spinach runs to seed too quickly to make it worth growing.

Herbs Grow a single row containing a few plants each of cilantro (leaf coriander), flat-leaved parsley, chives and other good leafy herbs for salad use.

MAKING THE MOST OF A SMALL SALAD BED

Left: Raised beds can also be used for a wide variety of vegetables. The deep soil means you can plant them closer together than usual – about half to two-thirds normal spacing. This means less work for you, as the plants smother out weeds, and you get more crops from the space. The vegetables planted here are kale, cabbage, cauliflower and kohl rabi, but you can grow any vegetables this way.

• Straight rows make the most of every bit of space, so use a cane laid across the top of the bed as a guide when sowing.
• Make your bed the same width as 'bought' cloches or rolls of horticultural fleece. Use these to cover crops for protection from the weather, so that you can make earlier spring sowings and keep late crops going longer than usual.
• Space rows of crops closer together. As the soil is deeper than in a normally prepared vegetable garden, the roots go down further.
• Sow alternate fast- and slow-growing crops, or upright and spreading crops (such as spring onions and lettuce). That way, you can reduce the spacing more, which means even greater productivity.
• As soon as one row of lettuces is almost ready for cutting, sow some more seeds in 'cell trays' or small pots so that the next

Above: Horticultural fleece acts like a cloche, bringing on salads sown or planted early in the season. Use it in autumn to protect late crops from cold weather. Drape it over the plants and bury the edges in soil to secure it.

batch of plants is ready to put in as soon as there is space for it. This way the bed stays full all the time and no space is wasted.

Transplanting seedlings

Grandpa's Tip

Sow little and often to avoid having masses of lettuces all ready at the same time. A pinch of seed every two weeks should be enough; it saves waste and also means you don't spend so much on seed. If you do grow too many at once, steam the hearts until tender and serve with peas in a creamy sauce as a cooked vegetable.

1 *Prepare an area of raised bed ready to receive the seedlings. Dig up the seedlings or tip them out of their pots and gently separate the clumps into single plants without damaging the leaves or roots.*

2 *Plant individual seedlings a suitable distance apart depending on the final size of the plants. These are rocket, which can be planted 7.5-10cm (3-4in) apart. Firm the soil gently around the roots and water.*

3 *Lettuces will grow 10-25cm (4-10in) across, depending on which variety they are, so plant them a suitable distance apart for the variety; see the back of the seed packet for instructions.*

4 *An intensive salad bed like this should be kept fully planted the whole time, but can still look quite decorative, given an edging of herbs. The plants here are coriander (looks like big parsley), green frilly basil 'Green Ruffles', purple non-frilly basil 'Dark Opal' and chives.*

Tomatoes in tubs

Raising something you can eat is one of the most satisfying of gardening experiences, and tomatoes are amongst the most rewarding crops. You can pick a few every day throughout late summer and early autumn – and home-grown tomatoes, ripened fully on the vine, taste far better than those that you buy. You don't need a greenhouse if you grow outdoor varieties; choose a warm sheltered spot – the plants look good enough to grow on the patio. Grow them in large tubs 30-38cm (12-15in) in diameter and stand them in front of a sunny wall, where they'll enjoy the reflected heat and light. This also makes the plants easy to support, as you can tie them up to a trellis or panel.

Above: Unusual varieties are available as seed or young plants from specialist seed firms in early spring. 'Old Ivory', a white, egg-shaped tomato, turns the colour of cream when ripe.

Keeping out of trouble

When grown outdoors, tomatoes are relatively free from problems, but watch for greenfly on young leaves and near the tips of shoots. Black circular patches at the base of the fruits indicate that the plants were allowed to dry out earlier on. Water them regularly, so that they don't alternate between too wet and too dry. Drying out is most common when plants are grown in containers, as they dry out faster than those grown in a border full of soil.

Above: Yellowish leaves with green veins are a sign that tomatoes are suffering from a shortage of magnesium. Regularly use a liquid tomato feed that contains magnesium.

Ripening tomatoes off the plant

At the end of the summer, when it starts getting cold at night, tomatoes ripen much more slowly, so pick off all the remaining fruit and take it indoors. Sort it into two piles. Small green tomatoes will never ripen, so are best fried or used to make chutney. Full-sized tomatoes can be encouraged to ripen if you place them in a large, loose, plastic bag with a ripe apple or banana and keep them in a cool dark place. The ethylene given off by the fruit makes tomatoes ripen in 7-10 days.

TYPES OF TOMATOES

Traditional round red tomatoes
For outdoor growing, look for bush varieties. They don't need to have their sideshoots removed like the more widely grown cordon varieties. They also look more decorative, as you can grow them in a tub with a rustic obelisk for support.

Cherry tomatoes
These have masses of intensely flavoured, bite-sized fruit, which are favourites with children and as snacks. They are amongst the fastest to ripen.

Beefsteak tomatoes
When sliced, the large, often rather misshapen, fruits are like 'tomato steaks', and ideal for sandwiches or grilling. However, being so big, the fruits are often slow to ripen.

Unusual coloured tomatoes
The colours available include yellow, white, green and stripy, as well as orange, pink, purple and brown. They look colourful, both on the table and while they are growing, and taste even better than they look.

Grandpa's Tip

Nip out the growing tip of outdoor tomato plants six to eight weeks before the first expected frost in your area. If the plants are prevented from growing taller, all their energy goes into swelling and ripening the existing partly developed crop of small green tomatoes. Topping also stops them producing new flowers that would not have time to set and produce usable fruit before the plants are killed by frost.

Outdoor tomatoes have quite a short growing season, so it's essential to start with good plants that don't waste time 'catching up'. Here's how to tell the good from the bad.

Flower buds

Bad plant
No flower buds visible. Leaves pale and anaemic-looking, with broken leaflets, yellow or brown edges or spots. Stem long and leggy, crooked or broken.

Good plant
Lower truss of flower buds already formed, ideally first flower just opening. Leaves a deep rich green. Stem straight and undamaged.

Growing tomatoes

1 *Fill a tub with potting mixture and plant the tomato quite deeply, so that the pair of long, narrow, seed leaves at the base of the plant (which don't look like normal tomato leaves) are flush with the surface of the potting mix.*

2 *Unless the pot is standing at the foot of a trellis, push a 1.5m (5ft) cane alongside the plant so that you can tie in the stem for support.*

Use soft string and tie it in a loose figure of eight so that the plant is not pulled in tightly towards the cane.

3 *Water lightly, just enough to settle the potting mixture around the plant's roots, and water sparingly until the first fruit starts to swell. Each week, tie the new growth up to the stake and nip out the sideshoots regularly, as shown here.*

Continuing care

If you are away a lot, don't risk tomatoes drying out; put in an automatic watering system. You can make a simple 'temporary' system by standing a bucket of water on a box and making a 'wick' out of a strip of cloth to hang over the side of the bucket. Bury the other end of the wick in the pot.

Fruit trees

You might think that fruit trees take up too much room in a small garden, but nowadays various compact forms are available. You can also train fruit trees into a wide range of space-saving shapes on fences or trellis, which makes them both decorative and productive as wall plants or garden dividers.

Scientific Stuff

For a crop to 'set', most fruit trees require another variety (and in some cases two) to cross-pollinate them. If there isn't another tree of the same species that flowers at the same time as yours within about 100 metres – maybe in a neighbour's garden – then you'll need to plant one. Consult the nursery to see which varieties will cross-pollinate each other. Ornamental crab apples have a long flowering season and cross-pollinate most varieties of apples. Otherwise, grow a self-fertile fruit variety, such as 'Greensleeves' apple, 'Conference' pear, 'Victoria' plum or 'Stella' cherry.

Below: 'John Downie' is a good pollinator for apple trees, and has its own crop of rosy crab apples in autumn that are decorative and make excellent crab apple jelly.

Below: Pears need warmer conditions than apples to grow well and ripen, so they are a good choice for espalier training against a wall. The pears shown here are 'Conference', which is one of the most reliable varieties for general use.

Above: Step-over apple trees are simply single-stemmed cordon trees grown horizontally. They make very pretty edges to beds and borders and you'll get several pounds of fruit from each one. This is 'Pixie'. Prune in late summer to shorten the sideshoots.

FITTING FRUIT TREES INTO A SMALL GARDEN

Dwarfing rootstocks The most popular fruit tree types are now available growing on dwarfing rootstocks. These keep the trees naturally dwarf and also encourage them to start flowering and fruiting when they are much younger than usual. This means you could plant a fruit tree instead of a flowering tree at the back of a border or as a specimen tree in the lawn, knowing it won't outgrow its welcome.

Genetic dwarfs Patio peaches and nectarines are available that are naturally small trees producing full-sized fruit. They are ideal for growing in pots on the patio.

Cordon-trained trees Instead of growing a conventional tree, buy cordon-trained apple or pear trees (which are grown on dwarfing rootstocks) and grow them against a post-and-wire support as a fruiting 'hedge', or over an arch or fruit tunnel.

Fan-trained trees You can buy trees of plums, nectarines and peaches trained in a fan shape to grow against a sunny wall. This helps to ripen the fruit, as well as saving space and looking good.

Espalier trees These have one main trunk with two tiers of branches growing out horizontally to make a flat tree. They can be grown against a wall or used as a living 'garden divider'.

Family trees These have one trunk, but each branch is a different variety of apple chosen to pollinate its neighbours. This way, you can enjoy a range of flavours and be certain of getting a good crop.

Growing a fruit tree in a pot

The best time to start is in spring, so that you have the whole growing season ahead of you. However, it is perfectly OK to buy a tree growing in a pot at the garden centre at any time during the summer – even when it is in flower or fruit – as long as you look after it well after planting. Buy a cordon-trained or small standard-shaped tree growing on a dwarfing rootstock, or choose a genetic dwarf patio peach tree, as here.

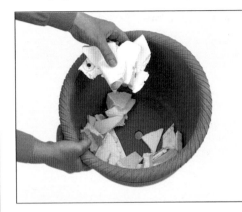 

1 *Stand a large 38-45cm (15-18in) pot or tub in a sheltered sunny spot; it will be too heavy to move later. Place a layer of broken clay flowerpot or polystyrene plant tray pieces in the bottom for drainage, or use a handful of pebbles.*

2 *Place a generous layer of soil-based potting mix in the bottom of the container, tip the fruit tree out of its pot and sit it in place. Put in a stake alongside the edge of the rootball so that it is 'planted' at the same time, with no risk of impaling the roots.*

3 *Use more potting mixture to fill the gap between the rootball and the edge of the pot. Firm the mixture gently down. Check that the top of the rootball is level with the surface of the potting mix; fruit trees should not be planted too deeply. Secure the trunk to the stake with a proper tree tie.*

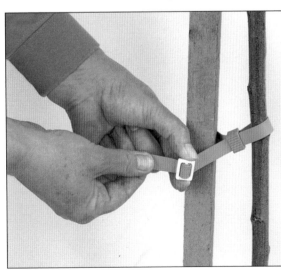

4 *Water well, and water regularly, so that the potting mix never dries out entirely. Use liquid tomato feed once a week, diluted at the rate recommended for tomatoes. During cold spells in winter, insulate the pot so that the potting mixture does not freeze solid. Make sure that the container is not standing in a puddle of water.*

Grandpa's Tip

You can tell when apples and pears are ready to pick by placing the flat palm of your hand underneath the fruit and lifting gently. If they come off, they are ready. Pick any apples and pears remaining on the tree in mid-autumn, otherwise windy weather will make them fall and bruise. Early varieties of apple are ready to eat in late summer, but they don't store. They are best picked and eaten straight off the tree.

Only attempt to store perfect, unblemished fruit. Use bruised fruit and windfalls straightaway, otherwise they will rot and infect any others close to them. You can keep apples and pears for several weeks in the salad drawer at the bottom of the fridge. Keep fruit for up to ten weeks in large, loose, plastic bags in a cool dark shed or garage.

Below: 'Victoria' plum is one of the most popular varieties, with heavy crops of large plums that can be eaten fresh or cooked. But unless you thin heavy crops, the tree will often 'miss' a year's fruiting.

A pebble pool

A pebble pool is perfect for anyone with a tiny garden or small children, or who is too busy to look after a water feature that needs regular upkeep. With a pebble pool, there is no standing water, just a low, bubbling fountain that runs away through the surrounding pebbles. You get all the sparkle, sound and water movement without the routine work or risks of a pond. Although pebble pools are popular for contemporary gardens, they can be landscaped to suit more traditional or even wilder styles of garden, just by altering the surroundings.

Anatomy of a pebble pool

Underground reservoir Water is endlessly recycled from the fountain into the reservoir. Clean it out once a year and refill it with fresh water.

Perforated lid This holds the weight of the pebbles. Because the water is kept in the dark most of the time, it will not become green as it would in a pond.

Fountain There's no need for a fountain nozzle; the top of the water pipe coming up from the pump produces a low, chunky bubble of water that suits a pebble pool and will not blow around in the wind.

Pebbles Not provided with the kit. Buy them in bags from garden centres for landscaping. Don't take them from the beach.

Pump Again, this is not included with the kit. A small pump is all you need.

Above: A millstone feature is a popular variation on the pebble pool theme. The water runs up through a hole in the middle, flows over the sides of the stone, between the pebbles and back into the underground reservoir.

Important – electrical safety

A lot of people are worried about having electrical wiring in the garden, especially where it is used in connection with water. Here's how to make sure you stay safe.
• Buy a low-voltage pump.
• Run the cable from the pebble pool to the nearest power point, which may be in a shed, garage or in the house. Run it through a length of hose or along the base of a wall or fence or the edge of a path. That way, you know where it is and it will be protected from accidental damage.
• Drill a hole through the wall and thread the cable through, connecting the plug on the other side.
• Plug it into the transformer that steps down the current, via a circuit breaker that cuts the power if the cable gets damaged.
• If in doubt, ask a qualified electrician to carry out the work for you.

Garden Doctor

Because there are no water plants in a pebble pool, you can position it anywhere in the garden – in sun or shade – but it's not a good idea to site it close to deciduous trees. Unless they are regularly cleared up, fallen leaves will make a mess of the pebbles, foul the water and clog the pump. But wherever you site the water feature, do surround it with suitable plants. In shade, hostas and ferns team well with a water feature.

Left: *This is a more complicated form of pebble pool, where the water from the overflowing jar runs over a tile 'cascade' and back into the reservoir under the pebbles. Installations such as this are best constructed by professionals, unless you are experienced at putting in water features.*

PLANTS TO PUT ROUND A PEBBLE POOL

• For a contemporary look in a sunny spot, surround the pebble pool with an irregular-shaped gravel area and put in architectural plants, such as phormium, occasional clumps of grassy-looking plants, such as sisyrinchium, carex, hakonechloa or bamboo, and an occasional chunk of rock.

• In light shade, go for a slightly more traditional look, using hostas, primulas, astilbe, hardy ferns and Bowles' golden grass if the soil stays moist.

• In a shadier corner, use *Fatsia japonica* with ivies, and euonymus with hardy cyclamen. Place a mirror behind squared trellis on the wall to reflect the light.

• To give more of a watery feel, grow waterloving plants, such as a tall cyperus and some floating water hyacinths or fairy moss, in a container standing to one side of the pebble pool.

Right: *If you don't have an electrical supply handy, you can still create a pebble pool effect just by filling a watertight container with water and pebbles. This looks good when it is partly tucked under plants.*

Installing a pebble pool

1 Dig a hole large enough to take the reservoir and line it with fine sand as 'cushioning'. Sink the reservoir into the ground and check that it is level. Sit the pump in the middle.

2 Put the lid on the reservoir, making sure that the pump outlet pokes up through the hole in the middle. Fill the reservoir with water and turn on the pump to check that all the water returns to the reservoir. If it splashes over the side, adjust the pump to reduce the height of the spray. Hide the reservoir lid under a layer of pebbles.

3 Put in suitable plants around the feature – ferns such as these, or hostas, astilbes and candelabra primulas look good with water, but dig plenty of organic matter into the ground around the pebble pool and keep the plants well watered, as the soil can be dry.

4 A bell jet produces an attractive-shaped spray, but don't put it in a windy area, otherwise the shape will be spoiled by the breeze. As water in the reservoir is lost by evaporation, top it up regularly to keep the pump submerged.

Growing climbers

Climbing plants are a good way of making the most of the upright elements of the garden — walls, fences and trellis — as well as vertical features, such as arches, pergolas and obelisks. You can be creative with climbers, growing them in containers on the patio or on a rustic wigwam or post in a border, where they make a novel feature that adds height without taking up much space. And if you want a speedy screen to make a new garden more private, then growing climbers over a trellis framework is much faster than planting a hedge. It also has the big advantage of not growing any taller than you want.

Scientific Stuff — How plants climb

In the wild, plants climb using trees as a means of support for their fast-growing shoots that seek the light, where they can flower and set seed. Climbers have several different methods of attaching themselves, which affect where we plant them in the garden.

- Self-clinging kinds grip onto hard surfaces, such as walls and tree trunks, using aerial roots in the case of ivies or 'suction cups' in the case of Virginia creeper.
- Scrambling kinds need something to hold onto, such as netting or trellis. Honeysuckle and wisteria twine round supports and will grow around a post, forming a 'head' at the top, rather like a small standard tree. Some scramblers hold onto twigs, etc., using tendrils, while clematis will loop their leaf stems round any handy support.
- Climbing roses hook downward-curving spines over twigs in trees. When they are grown on a wall, they need tying up to wires or trellis.
- Wall shrubs have to be trained to grow flat against the wall, but this is a good way to grow warmth-loving plants that need slight protection, such as ceanothus or fremontodendron. Wall training also looks decorative as a method of growing plants such as *Cotoneaster horizontalis*, pyracantha or chaenomeles (ornamental quince).

Think before you plant

- Don't plant self-clinging climbers on walls with cracked or crumbly mortar, as they can worsen the damage.
- In small gardens, avoid potentially large climbers such as wisteria. They need frequent cutting back, otherwise they take over.
- Wisteria stems thicken as they grow, so if trained on a house wall, don't allow them to wind round drainpipes or gutters, as they gradually force them away from the wall.

Left: Wisteria needs hard pruning every summer to stop it getting out of control, so grow it where you can get at it easily!

POPULAR CLIMBERS

Clematis Large flowered hybrids, such as 'Nelly Moser' have large, saucer-shaped flowers in summer. Plant on trellis or netting, so that the roots are in shade, but the tops can grow up into the sun. Prune hard in early spring or not at all, according to variety; see instructions on the plant label.

***Clematis alpina* varieties** Spring-flowering, with nodding, bell-shaped flowers. Grow on trellis or netting. No need to prune.

***Clematis montana* varieties** Large species with medium-sized, pink, rosette flowers in early summer. Good for growing along walls, on chain link fences or into trees. No pruning needed. 'Rubens' is pictured at right.

***Clematis texensis* and *viticella* varieties** Texensis have tulip-shaped flowers and those of viticella are small and rosette-like. They bloom in late summer and early autumn. These species are unaffected by wilt disease and good for growing through shrubs. No need to prune, but if grown on trellis, prune hard in spring to keep the plants compact.

Lonicera (honeysuckle) Scented, summer-flowering twiners, best for growing into trees or large shrubs. No need to prune.

Parthenocissus quinquefolia (Virginia creeper) and *P. tricuspidata* (Boston ivy) Huge, fast-growing, self-clinging climbers grown for brilliant autumn colour, but use them with care!

***Vitis vinifera* 'Purpurea'** *(purple grape vine)* Colourful, deciduous foliage and small bunches of sweet purple grapes. Good for growing on trellis teamed with clematis.

Wisteria Large, vigorous, early summer-flowering climbers. Normally grown on wires secured by 'vine eyes', which are long screws with an eyelet at the end.

Below: Fremontodendron 'California Glory' is a slow-growing, showy evergreen wall shrub with big waxy yellow flowers all summer. The hairs on the leaves can be an irritant, so handle the plant with care.

Above: Clematis viticella 'Alba Luxurians' has delicate flowers from midsummer to autumn. It is brilliant for growing through trees and big shrubs and doesn't need pruning.

Planting a climber

1 Dig a hole three to four times the size of the container the climber is growing in. If planting against a wall or tree, make the hole 45-90cm (18-36in) away from it.

2 Fork in at least one bucketful of well-rotted organic matter to improve the soil, which can often be very poor, especially close to a wall or a big tree.

3 Remove the climber from its pot and plant it inclined at an angle towards the wall or fence, or the tree or shrub it is to grow through. Most climbers should be planted so that the top of their rootball is level with the surrounding soil, but plant clematis so that the rootball is buried 10-15cm (4-6in) down. This way, it can regrow from underground buds if the base of the plant is damaged or attacked by clematis wilt.

4 For support, push in a cane or twiggy stem, also at an angle, and tie the stems closely up to it (right). When growing a climber into a big tree, plant it just under the outermost branches and tie a rope to a branch for the plant to grow up.

5 Fill in round the roots with a mixture of good-quality topsoil and well-rotted garden compost or manure. Firm gently and water well. Spread 5cm (2in) of compost or bark chippings all round to help the soil hold moisture. If the climber is growing in a situation where the soil dries out quickly, water it regularly every time the soil dries out for the whole of the first season. Dry soil is a common problem at the foot of a wall or close to a tree or large shrubs.

Growing grass

Despite the popularity of gravel and paving, grass will always be an important feature in most gardens. It is the green background that sets off everything else to perfection. The secret of good grass lies at its roots, with good preparation. Lawns need regular attention to keep them looking good, particularly small areas that are heavily used in summer as play areas.

Creating a new lawn

Soil preparation

Whether you are laying turf or sowing seed, first dig over the ground, remove any weeds and add as much well-rotted organic matter as you can spare. Sprinkle general-purpose fertiliser or a special pre-seeding lawn feed over the area and rake it in. Re-rake the area several times, removing stones and roots as you go. Firm down the soil evenly by treading it well with your feet, sinking your heels into soft spots. Then re-rake, leaving the surface smooth and level.

Laying turf

Turves measure approximately 90x30cm (36x12in) and are delivered rolled up; they should be laid or else opened out to the light within two to three days. Start at the end of the area closest to the stack of turf so that you don't walk over the prepared soil.

Place adjacent turves so that the cracks between them are staggered and they don't form long lines right across the lawn. Push turves up close together and firm down. Work in this way, right across the area,

SEED OR TURF?

There are two ways of growing a new lawn: either from seed or by laying turf. Seed is the cheapest method, but you must sow it in mid-spring or early autumn and it takes several months before the grass is fit to use. Turf costs more and takes longer to lay than sowing seed, but gives you a lawn that is ready to use within a few weeks. You can lay turf at any time from mid-autumn to spring, as long as the soil is in workable condition – not too wet or frozen. Turf laid in spring will need regular watering for most of the summer during spells of dry weather to enable it to establish properly.

Above: If you sow grass seed in autumn, the lawn has all winter to establish before you want to go out on it. By the following spring, you'll have a perfect lawn.

trimming the surplus turf around flower beds with an old carving knife. Standing on a plank as you work helps to keep the turves firmly in place and avoids leaving indentations on the grass.

Sowing seed

Sprinkle grass seed evenly over the prepared ground at the rate of 30-60gm per square metre (1-2oz per square yard). If you aren't sure how much this is, practise first on some

Laying turf to make a lawn

3 *Fill any gaps between the turves with fine soil and brush it in. This helps the turves knit together to make a complete grassy carpet, otherwise they look like crazy paving!*

1 *Unroll a row of turves to make a straight line along one end of the area and make sure the ends butt up closely together. Lay a plank over the first row of turf and stand on this to lay the second row. Don't walk on the raked, level soil, as you will leave footprints that make the grass uneven later.*

2 *As you work, gently firm down the turves with the back of a rake to ensure that the roots make good contact with the soil beneath. Don't ram them down too hard, however, as you don't want to over-compact the turf.*

Left: *A well-cared-for lawn that is regularly cut and has neatly trimmed edges sets off the whole garden.*

sheets of newspaper in the garage, or mark out the ground into squares using string or by sprinkling dry sand in lines. After sowing, rake the area thoroughly, but don't worry if you don't bury all the seed. Ignore the birds, as they won't eat much.

Aftercare

If it does not rain within 12 hours of sowing grass seed or laying turf, use a hose with a sprinkler attached to give the area a thorough soaking. Stand a straight-sided glass jar in the middle of the area to judge how much water has been put down; it should be at least 2.5cm (1in). If there is a long dry spell, repeat this procedure every three to seven days. Ideally, lay a new lawn when wet weather is forecast and then you won't need to water it.

Test the turf after two to three weeks by lifting a corner to see if it has started to root into the soil beneath. Give the grass its first cut once this has happened. You can then begin using the lawn, but avoid playing strenuous games on it to start with.

When grass seed germinates, the result looks very patchy at first and lots of weeds will appear; don't worry, as this is normal, but don't use fertiliser or weedkiller at this stage. When the longest grass is 7.5cm (3in) high, top it gently using sharp shears, which will take the top off without tearing the grass or pulling it up. A week or two later, use a hover mower with the blades set as high as possible to top the grass again. From then on, mow normally but not too short – about 3.2cm (1.25in). Any upright weeds will soon disappear as they can't re-grow when they are cut off regularly. Don't use lawn products such as weedkillers for at least six months.

Mowing

Grass grows whenever the soil temperature is over about 5°C (40°F), so mow each time the lawn starts to look shaggy, regardless of the time of year. As a general rule, mowing once a week in summer and once a month in winter is usually about right.

Don't cut the grass too short. A height of 1.25cm (0.5in) may be fine for a bowling green that is completely level and perfectly maintained, but it is much better to cut an ordinary garden lawn 2.5-3.2cm (1-1.25in)

Grandpa's Tip

Grass will remain green longer in dry conditions if you leave it longer than usual, so reset your mower blades to cut at 3.75cm (1.5in) in dry weather. And don't feed the lawn to try to get it growing again. Wait until the following spring, when it has had time to recover naturally.

high. This way, the grass stays greener and is less prone to problems. It also makes any bumps and hollows less noticeable, as you don't 'scalp' the hillocks.

Don't cut long grass short all in one go. If you've left the lawn uncut all winter or have just come back from a holiday, long grass will turn yellow if you suddenly cut it closely. Instead, raise the blades to their highest position for the first cut, then gradually reduce them a little at a time so that you cut the grass slightly shorter each time over the next few weeks.

Use a grass box if you like a neat finish, and feed the lawn regularly. However, it is much quicker to cut the grass if you don't use a grass box, as you don't have to keep stopping to empty it. In this case, mow little and often so that the clippings are short and quickly disappear into the turf instead of being trodden indoors. By leaving the clippings to recycle themselves back into the soil, they return nutrients to the lawn so that you do not have to feed it so often.

Above: *After mowing the lawn, trim round the edges where it butts up to paths and flower beds to finish the job neatly. You can use edging shears or a rotary line trimmer with an adjustable head that turns through 90°, specially designed to do lawn edging.*

Above: *This is a combined feed-and-weed treatment, but don't apply it until the worst of the frosts are over and the weather is mild.*

Weeds

Upright weeds, such as groundsel, and even troublesome perennial weeds, such as nettles and thistles, quickly disappear once you start mowing. Upright weeds growing in an established lawn are a sign of poor lawn condition. Feeding the grass and mowing more often gets rid of them easily.

Remove rosette weeds such as daisy and dandelion using a daisy grubber, or spot-treat them with aerosol lawn weedkiller.

Treat large weedy areas with a combined feed-and-weed lawn treatment. Tackle small-leaved weeds such as trefoils in fine weather in late spring before they start to flower, using a liquid weedkiller specifically aimed at small-leaved lawn weeds. Repeat at two-weekly intervals.

Moss

Tackle moss in spring. You can rake it out by hand, use a powered lawn raking machine or apply a proprietary moss killer. Some kinds also kill liverworts and green algae, which cause the surface of the lawn to become slimy in a wet winter. Unless the problem has been caused by an unusually wet winter, moss normally creeps back slowly, so annual treatment is often needed.

TIME AND MONEY SAVERS

If the lawn has weeds or moss that need treatment, you can buy all-in-one lawn care products that contain a feed and a treatment, saving you both time and money.
Look out for modern slow-release lawn feeds. If used in late spring, they have a 'little-and-often' effect right through the season. Although they are a bit more expensive, they are ideal for hard-wearing family lawns.

Hedges

Hedges are much more than tough practical boundaries for country areas; now, decorative hedges are being used to divide gardens into fashionable 'outdoor rooms'. Even small town gardens often include stylish formal features, such as a herb bed or knot garden outlined with dwarf hedges.

HEDGE CLIPPING EQUIPMENT

Single-handed shears or sheep shears
Brilliant for clipping topiary or dwarf hedges around formal flower beds, but too small for serious hedge clipping.

Hedging shears
The traditional choice; slow and tiring, but good if you only have small areas to cut, especially low hedges.

Cordless trimmers
Quick and easy to use as you don't have to worry about cables, but they don't hold enough charge to cut a lot of hedge before they need recharging.

Electric hedge-trimmers
Make light work of cutting larger hedges so long as cables are within reach of a power point.

Petrol hedge-cutters
The most powerful and expensive; useful for tough jobs or hedges beyond the reach of an electric cable, but heavy and tiring to use due to vibration, and not necessary in most gardens.

Above: Hedges don't just make effective boundaries; they are also good for outlining borders and making a leafy, year-round backdrop for garden architecture.

Left: You can clip peepholes, arches and windows in hedges for a bit of variety or to open up a pleasant view from the house.

Below: Dwarf hedges such as lavender make a good formal flowering feature. Clip them lightly after they have flowered.

Grandpa's Tip

If you like the look of a hedge but don't want the regular work involved in keeping it clipped, plant a screen instead. You can use a row of bamboos or any reasonably compact, evergreen or strongly upright-growing small trees. Check that their ultimate height is acceptable, and you won't have to do any clipping.

You can also convert wire netting or chain link fencing into a 'hedge' by planting evergreen climbers along it. They'll soon hide the mesh and won't grow any taller than the height of the structure they are growing on.

What hedge where?

Country area with livestock next door Hawthorn or holly.
Mixed country hedge to attract wildlife *Acer campestre*, blackthorn, dog rose, elder, hazel, hawthorn and holly.
Windy area *Rosa rugosa*.
Formal evergreen hedges Box or yew.
Low conifer/evergreen hedging to clip Thuja, *Viburnum tinus*.
Clipped country garden hedges Beech or hornbeam.
Seaside Clipped *Escallonia macrantha*, an informal row of *Griselinia littoralis* or sea buckthorn (*Hippophae rhamnoides*).

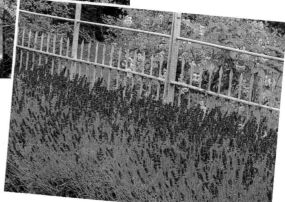

Dwarf hedges
Dwarf box (*Buxus sempervirens* 'Suffruticosa'), hebe, lavender, rosemary, santolina.
Flowering hedges Forsythia, *Prunus cistena*, *Prunus pissardii* 'Pissardii Nigra', shrub roses.
Prickly hedges to deter intruders/pets Berberis, pyracantha, species roses.

Designer's Tip

• It's not easy to clip a hedge straight 'by eye', so knock in a post at each end of the hedge and run a taut string along it to use as a guide.

• When you clip a hedge, angle the sides very slightly so that the top is narrower than the base. As well as making the hedge more stable, the base won't be in as much shade, and more rain will be able to reach the roots. This way, the bottom will stay green instead of dying out, as often happens.

• If you have a tall hedge, don't risk using power tools above your head, and don't reach out from the top of wobbly step-ladders. Either reduce the hedge to a manageable height, invest in a proper portable platform from which to work, or call in a professional garden maintenance firm who have the right equipment.

• Wear goggles to reduce the risk of dust or flailing twigs damaging your eyes when hedge-trimming.

Above: *Tall hedges are best cut by standing on a firm, safe platform. Don't try to work holding hedge clippers above your head!*

Planting a hedge

For an economical hedge, buy common hedging plants, such as beech, hawthorn ('quick') and hornbeam seedlings, which are sold cheaply in bundles with bare roots in winter. Soak the roots in water for a couple of hours to rehydrate the plants if they have been standing for a while and plant them within 24 hours.

1 *Hedging and screening plants are often sold in bundles with bare roots in winter, because this keeps down the cost when you need to buy a lot of them. Keep the roots moist and only separate them when you are about to plant.*

2 *Dig a trench 30cm (12in) wide and deep where the hedge is to go, and put in as much well-rotted organic matter as you can spare. Fork it well into the bottom of the trench, then sprinkle general-purpose fertiliser along its length and mix in.*

3 *Space the plants 30cm (12in) apart in a double staggered row. Cut them back to 5cm (6in) above ground after planting.*

4 *After planting, water well and then mulch. To help a new hedge establish quickly, feed and water it for the first season.*

Continuing care

Trim a new formal hedge regularly until it reaches the required height. To shape and thicken the plants, clip them lightly each time they grow 5cm (2in). Just take the tips off the ends of the shoots, so the hedge can continue to grow taller. This ensures that it makes a good, solid wall of interlocking twigs with foliage right down to the ground, instead of a loose, gappy hedge that splays apart and has gaping holes along the base. For a more ornamental hedge or to create

immediate impact, buy shrubs growing in pots at a garden centre. These can be planted at any time of year except when the soil is unworkable due to freezing or very wet weather. A single row is normally enough in the case of conifers or compact shrubs, but if you want a tall hedge (laurel and escallonia are good choices here), plant a staggered row to give the hedge more stability. Choose bushy plants with plenty of growth at the base.

Fences

Fences say a lot about the style of your garden, so make sure they put over the right message. There are so many different kinds available, and not just for enclosing the garden; use decorative panels as supports for climbers or on their own as screens to give the garden shape and character. Nowadays, you don't have to settle for natural woody shades; colours are popular, too.

Left: For a perennial climber that won't grow too big, try Ampelopsis brevipedunculata 'Elegans'. The three-coloured mini 'vine' type leaves are a picture from summer to autumn.

Left: Clematis viticella 'Etoile Violette' is a popular variety that flowers from midsummer to autumn, adding welcome colour to a fence. Like all Clematis viticella varieties, it is safe from the clematis wilt disease that sometimes affects other kinds.

Grandpa's Tip

People often choose fences when they really want a hedge, because a fence is instant and they would have to wait for a hedge to grow. But you can have the best of both worlds if you use an inexpensive fence, such as wire netting tacked to a row of posts, to enclose the garden at the same time as you plant a hedge just inside it. The fence provides shelter and protection for the plants, and when they are big enough, you can take the fence down. Better still, let the hedge grow through it to provide internal reinforcement and to make the hedge totally impenetrable to pets, people or livestock.

FENCING PANELS

Interwoven panels
Popular 'first fences', as they are relatively cheap and easily available. However, the thin strips of timber quickly become brittle and are easily vandalised or broken.

Trellis panels
Very adaptable and can be nailed to posts to make various shapes or open-sided garden buildings. Put trellis on top of a low wall to give a garden more privacy. Modern versions with scalloped tops make novel garden screens.

Traditional styles
These include picket fences, which have alternating wooden uprights and gaps, and close-boarded fences, which are solid walls of wood. If using them as a garden boundary, make sure that gates or arches match.

Hurdles
Made of woven hazel and originally used as temporary enclosures for sheep. You can now buy rustic panels of willow or heather. They are very fashionable and, like hazel hurdles (below), are quick to put up, as there is no need to cement in strong posts. Use panels of textured natural materials to cover the side of an unsightly outbuilding or an old fence and turn it into something more interesting.

70

Fence maintenance

Natural wood fences need treating with timber preservative every one or two years. Try to do this in winter, when early plants are dormant and perennials are still underground, to avoid drops splashing onto them. Plant-friendly wood preservatives are the safest to use; otherwise cover nearby plants with large fabric or plastic sheets.

Coloured wood preservative stains are popular now. The most economical method of applying these types of product is with a brush, but for small areas or complicated shapes, aerosol versions are quicker and easier to use.

Painted fences are the trickiest to deal with, as it is essential that all the surfaces are protected. If not, damp can get in and the timber can start to rot from the inside. Use good-quality, exterior-grade gloss paint, and rub down any loose or flaky areas before repainting them. If fence posts rot off at the base, or arris rails (the horizontal fence struts that are triangular in cross section) rot at the ends, there is no need to replace a whole panel. You can repair them using special metal posts or brackets.

Below: Attractive fencing can be teamed with other garden features to carry through the same style of decoration. Don't just put fencing around the edge of the garden; use it to create special theme areas or 'rooms' within it, too.

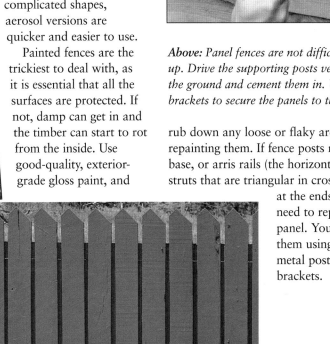

Above: Panel fences are not difficult to put up. Drive the supporting posts vertically into the ground and cement them in. Use panel brackets to secure the panels to the posts.

Left: Fences can be a 'fashion statement', depending on whether you go for a natural look or a bright colour. Use fencing to shelter a seating or barbecue area while you wait for plant borders to grow.

Garden Doctor – Growing climbers on fences

When you grow climbers over a wooden fence, remember that periodically you will need to get at the timber to paint it with preservative or to make repairs. Either grow annual climbers, such as morning glory, or the sort that can be cut back close to the ground every year or two, such as some types of clematis, or *Ampelopsis brevipedunculata* 'Elegans', which often dies back to the ground in cold winters. (But don't worry; it grows back again the following year.) Otherwise, grow climbers on panels of trellis or rigid, plastic-covered netting held a short distance away from the fence by wooden blocks used as spacers. That way, you can lift down the entire climber and its supports while you work on the fence. Lay a plastic sheet over the climber while you apply preservative so that it won't come to any harm. Be sure to give the substance several days to dry and air thoroughly before reinstating both the climber and its support.

Above: Gardens need to look good all year round. Evergreens give the garden 'shape', while temporary hot-spots bring out each season in turn. Here, euphorbia, early summer bulbs, Judas tree foliage and allium provide summer colour.

Part Three

Regular garden care

A garden is a living thing, so don't expect it to stay the same as when you originally planted it. Just as everything starts to mature and look perfect, it grows and changes. You can't just leave it alone to look after itself. It needs a little regular attention to keep everything looking its best. Aim to spend a couple of hours every week doing routine chores in spring and summer, and that way you'll keep on top of a small garden quite easily. It takes much longer to get the garden back into shape if you neglect it for very long just when everything is growing its fastest. Little and often is the secret of easy gardening. Then you will still have time to relax and enjoy what you have created.

Common problems

Even the best-kept gardens are not without their problems. But not everything that can go wrong with plants is due to pests or diseases; the weather, physical damage and cultural faults can all cause trouble. Running a successful garden means anticipating, identifying and dealing with problems in time, instead of letting small problems grow bigger.

Left: Typical snail damage on a hosta leaf. Snails eat the soft tissues and leave the ribs. These attractive plants are a favourite snail snack!

Left: Hunt for snails at night by going out into the garden with a torch. They hide away during the day to avoid being dehydrated by the heat of the sun.

Pests

Slugs and snails come out at night and rasp at plant foliage, causing typical 'threadbare' patches. Snails are worst in areas with chalky soil, as they need lime to manufacture their shells, and unlike slugs they can climb walls and plants to reach leaves to feed on.
REMEDY: If slug pellets are used, follow the directions carefully and spread pellets very thinly. To protect pets and wildlife, don't pile them up in heaps. Otherwise, gather slugs and snails by hand and put down saucers of beer as slug traps.
MOST AT RISK: Soft foliage, such as lettuces and hostas.
FOUND: In damp, shady places under plants, in crevices and under stones.

Greenfly feed by perforating soft young tissues to suck sap. Unless there is a bad infestation on a young plant they don't do much damage, but they can spread viruses between plants by 'injecting' them as they feed. Their sticky secretions also attract ants, which may 'farm' greenfly, and encourage sooty mould, which grows on the sugary coating left behind on leaves where greenfly have been feeding.

Above: To control the black bean aphid naturally, nip out the growing tips of the shoots of broad beans once a good crop has 'set'.

Left: Greenfly (green aphids) are mainly found on shoot tips, young leaves and flower buds, as the tissues are thinner there and it is easier for them to feed.

REMEDY: Spray with selective aphid killer to avoid harming beneficial creatures. You can wipe them off with your fingers or a damp cloth – or leave them for the birds!
MOST AT RISK: Roses, young plants.
FOUND: At the tips of stems, flower buds and on young leaves.

Blackfly (black aphids) gather in large numbers on the young shoots of certain plants, but don't affect others at all.
REMEDY: Spray with selective aphid killer or remove by hand. Cut off affected stems where appropriate.
MOST AT RISK: Sambucus (elder) and broad beans, which are very prone to attack by black bean aphid.
FOUND: At the tips of young stems.

Vine weevil are small brownish-grey beetles with a Y-shaped 'antenna' at the front. The adults take scallop-shaped 'bites' from the edges of evergreen leaves, particularly rhododendrons, but the larvae are the biggest problem. They gnaw roots; affected plants wilt and turn yellow, then collapse and die quite suddenly.
REMEDY: New pesticides are available that you water onto the soil or around at-risk plants. A biological control and potting mixture pretreated with pesticide are other alternatives.
MOST AT RISK: Primula, cyclamen and plants growing in containers.
FOUND: Look for grubs around the roots of the plants mentioned above and in pots of any peaty planting mixtures.

Soil pests, such as leatherjackets, cutworms and wireworms, are the underground larvae of various beetles and 'daddy longlegs'. They feed on plant roots, causing young plants to turn yellow suddenly and wither.
REMEDY: Treat newly cultivated ground with soil pesticide or dig it over several times in winter to expose grubs to the birds.
MOST AT RISK: Newly planted vegetables and flowers.
FOUND: Anticipate that soil pests may be a problem on newly cultivated soil that was previously grassland. They are also common in vegetable gardens.

Above: Cutworms (top), wireworms (left) and chafer grubs (centre) are three very common soil pests that chew off plant roots.

Diseases

Powdery mildew is a fungal disease that looks like talcum powder on plant foliage. It is most common in late summer and early autumn, when the daytime conditions are warm and humid and the nights are colder.

Above: Powdery mildew often affects roses, especially after a dry spell. Mulch heavily in spring. Water in dry spells to avoid problems.

REMEDY: Spray regularly with fungicide or grow disease-free varieties of at-risk plants. Control weeds; they often harbour spores.
MOST AT RISK: Roses, Michaelmas daisies.
FOUND: On the upper sides of young foliage and around the tips of shoots and flower buds.

Rust disease looks like dull, red-brown spots on foliage.
REMEDY: No real cure once established, so destroy affected foliage to prevent spreading. Spray roses with fungicide.

MOST AT RISK: Roses, leeks and pelargoniums. (Different strains of rust affect each; they don't spread from one kind of plant to another.)
FOUND: On foliage.

Above: Rust looks like red or brown dots that spread to make larger patches. Use a special rose fungicide regularly if this is a problem.

Grey mould spreads fast in damp, overcrowded conditions, such as are found in tubs and hanging baskets during dull, damp summers. It can affect foliage and flowers, turning them to grey fluff.
REMEDY: Pick off dead leaves and dead-head plants regularly to avoid the problem.
MOST AT RISK: Tomatoes, plants in greenhouses and conservatories.
FOUND: Mainly on dying flowers and leaves, but can affect living tissue on any part of the plant.

Brown rot causes concentric rings of raised white spots growing in soft, brown, rotten patches on fruit, such as apples. It mainly affects windfall fruit on the ground, but where spores are present, they can cause fruit still on the tree to rot if the weather is warm and humid, with cold nights.
REMEDY: None. Gather and destroy affected fruit to limit the spread of spores.

Right: Some roses always have problems with fungal diseases, and regular spraying is the only remedy. If you prefer not to use sprays, dig out these plants and replace them with disease-resistant varieties.

MOST AT RISK: Apples, pears, crab apples, quinces.
FOUND: On mature fruit in late summer and autumn.

Frost damage

Frost damage affects even perfectly hardy plants if they have been encouraged to start growing by mild spring weather that is then followed by a late frost. Leaves may turn black, curly or wrinkled, and if killed off, new growth may be slow to appear. Early blossom may also be killed, which can mean loss of fruit crops.
REMEDY: If late frost is forecast, cover at-risk plants with horticultural fleece. To treat affected plants, wait until new growth appears and then cut back dead shoot tips just above healthy new growth.
MOST AT RISK: Fruit tree blossom and early-flowering plants growing in exposed situations or where they receive early morning sun. This thaws out frozen buds, etc., too quickly, causing the cells to collapse.
FOUND: On blossom, young foliage or the tips of young shoots.

Grandpa's Tip

Don't spray plants that are under stress due to heat or lack of water. Don't spray open flowers during the day when bees are about. Always follow the instructions on the product and never be tempted to exceed the stated dose. Don't use on susceptible plants (listed in the instructions), as damage may result.

If using a hand sprayer or ready-to-use sprayer pack, thoroughly spray both sides of the leaves until the droplets join together and start to run off the plant.

If using an aerosol, spray lightly from arm's length and don't attempt to cover the plant in droplets.

The organic alternative

If you don't like the idea of using chemical pesticides, weedkillers and fertilisers in the garden, there are plenty of natural alternatives, including several modern labour-saving devices that are suitable for organic gardeners.

Organic seed and potting mixtures

Peat-free mixtures based on coir or composted manure are sometimes available in garden centres, but are most easily obtained by mail order from a specialist supplier of organic gardening goods. You can make your own mixture using sterilised soil, plus some completely rotted organic material, such as leafmould or coir (fine coconut husk), and base fertiliser, available from garden centres specially for use in homemade potting mixes. However, it does take time, and results can be variable.

Above: Pelleted chicken manure makes a valuable, general organic feed for use all round the garden, but it is especially good for vegetables.

To sterilise soil, take some good, loamy topsoil and allow it to dry out partially in a tray in the shed. Loosely fill a large, oven-roasting bag and place it in the oven on the lowest heat for at least one hour. Small soil sterilisers are sometimes available from specialist catalogues, and these are more convenient for larger quantities.

To make leafmould, pile the dead leaves of deciduous trees into a cage made by hammering four posts into the ground and nailing wire netting round them. Dampen each layer as you add it, and leave for one year until it has completely broken down and looks like rich soil. Oak and beech leaves take up to two years to decompose. Then sterilise as for soil, before adding to potting mixtures.

FERTILISERS AND GROWTH BOOSTERS

Pelleted chicken manure
Blood, fish and bone
Liquid seaweed extract

SOIL IMPROVERS

Garden compost
Manure produced from non-intensive systems
Composted bark

Grandpa's Tip

Instead of killing grass with weed-killer when you make a new bed in a lawn, skim off the turf in 2.5cm (1in)-thick oblongs and stack them upside down in a heap. Cover with a sheet of black plastic and leave for six months. When you uncover it, it will have turned to good-quality topsoil that you can use for topdressing beds or as loam for homemade potting compost.

Above: A compost heap should contain plenty of different materials in 7.5-15cm (3-6in) layers, sandwiched together.

Above: Covering vegetable crops such as cabbage and lettuce with very fine plastic mesh, screens out insect pests such as greenfly without needing to spray them. It also protects them from pigeons and larger pests. Don't use horticultural 'fleece' for pest protection, as it causes crops to overheat in summer.

Anti-pest precautions

A wide range of safe, non-toxic pest deterrents is available by mail order from specialist organic suppliers.

● To keep out insect pests, cover at-risk vegetable crops, such as carrots or members of the cabbage family, with very fine, insect-proof netting from sowing or planting right through to harvesting.

● Drape biodegradable fibrous threads over fruit bushes and strawberries to discourage birds. This is much safer than netting, in which birds can become entangled.

● Choose varieties of plants or seeds with in-bred resistance to pests or disease. This applies especially to roses, tomatoes and vegetables.

● Use sonic devices to repel moles or cats harmlessly. They emit sound waves that humans cannot hear.

● Sulphur sprays or powders make good fungicides for general use.

● Soft soap solutions are sold specially for use as organic pesticides.

● Pick off caterpillars by hand or wipe off aphids with a damp cloth where they appear in quantities, or simply leave pests for natural predators to feed on.

● String 'humming line' or rows of old tin cans on threads across seedbeds or soft fruit to deter birds.

Make your own soil improver

1 *A compost bin is the most reliable way of getting rubbish to rot down quickly, and is the most suitable method for a small garden. Stand the bin on a level surface after forking over the soil to loosen it slightly.*

2 *If you have large amounts of one type of material, such as lawn mowings, add them in 15cm (6in)-deep layers, alternated with other materials. Firm down loose material and dampen dry material with the hose after adding it.*

3 *Fill the bin to the top, then cap it with a layer of soil, put on the lid and leave until the ingredients look like soil. This usually takes three months in summer and six months in winter. Don't add more material during this time.*

4 *Empty the bin and use the contents for mulching borders, digging in to improve soil, or before planting.*

You can add kitchen waste, such as outer leaves, peelings and vegetable trimmings, but not meat or cooked food, which attract rodents.

Left: Unless you only have small amounts of garden rubbish, it is worth having two compost bins – one to fill, while the other rots down. This way you are not tempted to add new material to a heap that is nearly ready to use.

Weeds

Flame gun Use a small, gas-powered flame gun to clear vacant ground. Repeat after 14 days to burn off dead tops, and again two weeks later if there is any regrowth from the roots of perennial weeds. Well-established weeds may need several regular treatments; don't allow them to recover between times.

Hoeing Hoe regularly between rows of vegetables to disturb germinating weeds before they grow big enough to need hand-weeding. Hoe on a sunny day when the soil surface is dry, so that uprooted weeds shrivel up and die. Otherwise, rake them up to prevent re-rooting.

COMPOST INGREDIENTS
Annual weeds
Vegetable garden trimmings
Dead leaves
Old bedding plants at the end
of the season
Soft hedge clippings
Lawn clippings
Kitchen peelings
Soiled litter from hutches of
rabbits, guinea pigs and hamsters
Plain white paper
Natural cotton or woollen fabric

DON'T USE
Weeds with seed heads
Roots of perennial weeds
Diseased material
Tough stems, unless first
chopped up into small pieces
Prunings or twigs

Garden Doctor – Slugs and snails

Natural remedies for slugs and snails enable you to tackle these troublesome pests without resorting to slug pellets.
• Set out dishes of beer around the garden at night, then tip the drowned slugs onto the compost heap each morning and refill the dishes.
• Grow at-risk plants, such as hostas, in containers and smear crop protection jelly around the pot rims.

• Place special copper tape round vegetable beds. This releases a minute electrical charge when slugs and snails cross it, acting like an electric fence.
• Go out at night with a torch and collect up slugs and snails by hand.
• In winter, snails congregate in large clusters under rubble and piles of pots to hibernate. By hunting them then, you can eliminate large numbers before they come out looking for a meal in spring.

Above: When putting down beer traps for slugs, set the saucer with the rim slightly above soil level, so that ground beetles (which are beneficial to the garden) won't fall in.

Beneficial creatures

Control pests the natural way by encouraging beneficial creatures to visit your garden to feed. They'll arrive all on their own when you stop using chemicals and provide them with a safe environment. And it's amazing how much good they can do, besides being fun to watch.

Right: Nestboxes are a good way to encourage birds to colonise the garden. Put them up in winter so that the birds can get used to them well before the start of the breeding season.

Below: Blend insect-friendly flowers into an informal perennial border or plant them into gaps between shrubs if you don't have a separate wildlife garden.

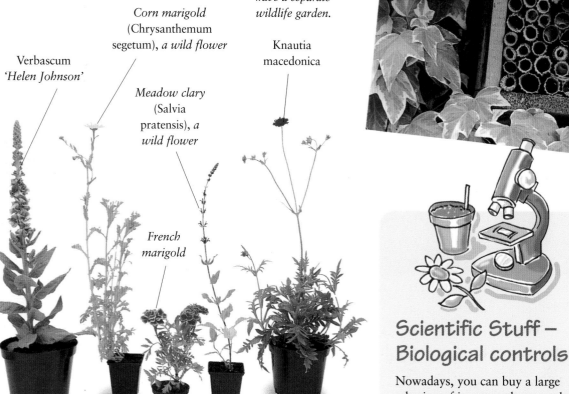

Verbascum 'Helen Johnson'

Corn marigold (Chrysanthemum segetum), *a wild flower*

Meadow clary (Salvia pratensis), *a wild flower*

Knautia macedonica

French marigold

Above: Insect houses made of slices of hollow plant stems provide safe overwintering chambers for beneficial lacewings.

Scientific Stuff – Biological controls

Nowadays, you can buy a large selection of insect predators and parasites to tackle both indoor and outdoor pests. Biological controls for greenfly and whitefly are most effective used in a heated greenhouse in spring. Those for vine weevil and slugs in the garden are best used in late spring. As they are living organisms they cannot be stored, so buy them by mail order or via garden centres and use them straightaway. Follow the directions carefully.

Right: Many bird species benefit the garden. Song thrushes are natural predators of snails, using stones as 'anvils' to crack open the hard shells or smashing them on paths.

Water garden tips

Keep goldfish in an ornamental pond close to the house. They will feed on midge and mosquito larvae that live in the water, and help to keep down the number of biting insects when you want to sit out in the garden on summer evenings.

Where there is room for two ponds, encourage frogs and toads to colonise a wilder pond further down the garden by moving their spawn to it from your fish pond. Both frogs and toads consume large numbers of slugs and other garden pests.

ATTRACTING NATURAL PREDATORS TO THE GARDEN

Left: Hedgehogs are well worth encouraging into the garden, as they eat large numbers of slugs and snails.

Birds

Robins feed on soil pests and often follow gardeners when they dig over a piece of ground. Bluetits take large numbers of greenfly in spring and summer, while thrushes crack open snail shells. Blackbirds consume quantities of small caterpillars. Provide nestboxes and twiggy trees, and feed birds in winter.

Frogs and toads

Adults feed on slugs and other pests. Put in a small pond with sloping sides so that both adults and young can get in and out easily.

Foxes

Not everyone regards foxes as beneficial creatures, but their regular presence discourages rabbits and rodents, and they feed on snails and other garden pests.

Spiders

Between them, spiders are some of the most effective predators in the garden; even tiny money spiders take huge numbers of aphids.

Grandpa's Tip

It doesn't matter if you don't know the names of creepy-crawlies, as long as you remember the old rule of thumb: if it moves slowly, step on it, but if it moves fast, spare it. This works because slow-moving creatures are usually ones that eat plants – which aren't going to run away – while fast-moving creatures live by chasing slower creatures, which are likely to be vegetarian.

Hedgehogs

Hedgehogs are one of the few garden predators that can tackle snails, but they also take slugs and other pests. Avoid moving piles of rubbish or compost heaps in winter, as you may disturb hibernating hedgehogs. Bury wooden boxes under mounds of dead leaves for them in autumn. Encourage hedgehogs by putting out tinned cat food, but don't give them saucers of milk, as it upsets their stomachs.

Shrews

Shrews look like tiny bottle-nosed mice. They often nest in large family groups in compost heaps in winter, but unlike most rodents, they are carnivorous and feed on slugs and snails, gnawing characteristic holes in the middle of the spiral of a snail shell to get to the contents. Leave compost heaps undisturbed for them to live in until they move away in late spring.

Ladybirds

Familiar small, red beetles with black spots. Both adults and larvae consume large numbers of aphids. Avoid disturbing hibernating groups in loose debris under hedges and in similar places.

Above: Most people recognise the ladybird, but its larvae, also seen here, are not so well known. They are valuable aphid-eaters.

Above: Violet ground beetles are not violet at all, but a shiny black colour, and like other similar species feed on all sorts of harmful creatures such as slugs.

Beetles

A wide variety of black beetle species clear large numbers of soil pests. Place fibre 'collars' around members of the cabbage family in the vegetable garden. Beetles live under them and feed on cabbage root fly.

Hoverflies

Both adults and larvae feed on aphids. Encourage adults by planting nectar-rich flowers. Provide overwintering chambers for them, such as sections of hollow bamboo.

Earwigs

These live in crevices in bark. Although often mistaken for pests, they feed on fruit tree pests and overwintering insect eggs.

Weeds and weeding

'Weeds' are any plants that are growing in the wrong place. The commonest weeds are fast-growing native plants that spread quickly from seed, such as groundsel, or by rampant underground root systems, such as bindweed. However, some cultivated garden plants can reach plague proportions when they seed or spread themselves too freely. If there's a big tree nearby, you might also find that saplings such as sycamore are a recurrent problem in borders, and for the first few years after rough ground is first cultivated, you often find grass and tough perennial weeds reappearing unless the problem is tackled right from the start.

Left: The most effective way to get rid of buttercup (left), dock (centre) and nettles (right), without using weedkiller is to dig them out along with all their roots. Don't put them onto the compost heap.

Below right: Annual weeds such as groundsel are easily dealt with by regular hoeing, but do it before they flower and set seed.

PERENNIAL WEEDS
These have longlived roots so, although they die down in winter, they come up again every year unless you get them right out.
Bindweed
Buttercup
Couch grass
Dock
Ground elder
Horsetail
Nettles
Thistles

ANNUAL WEEDS
These flower, shed their seed and die within a single growing season.
Charlock
Fat hen
Groundsel
Hairy bittercress
Knotgrass
Mayweed
Poppy
Shepherd's purse

Grandpa's Tip

There's an old saying that goes 'one year's seeds, seven years weeds', and it's true. When a weed sheds its seeds, they don't all germinate at the same time like flower seeds do. Instead, they come up a few at a time over the next few years, so at least some of their seedlings avoid natural disasters. That explains why weeds are such good survivors!

What's wrong with weeds?

The trouble with weeds is that, being wild, they grow faster than cultivated plants – which are bred for characteristics such as colour and beauty, not for vigour – and quickly swamp them. When light cannot reach the leaves, cultivated plants die. It's not just soft plants, such as annuals, that are affected; dense weed growth can even smother out big, tough shrubs if it is left to grow up over them. Even small weeds compete with cultivated plants for water, nutrients and growing space, as well as harbouring all kinds of pests and diseases; slugs and snails love weedy gardens. And apart from anything else, weeds make a garden look neglected.

GETTING TO GRIPS WITH WEEDS

Left: When hoeing, the art is to disturb only the very surface of the soil so that new layers of weed seeds are not brought to the surface, where they'll germinate because of the light.

Right: A 'trickle bar' fitted to the spout of a watering can lets you treat a wider area, perfect for applying path weedkiller.

nearby plants with card or cover them with plastic sheet or an upturned bucket.
WHAT TO USE: Systemic products based on glyphosate.
WHEN TO SPRAY: When weeds are growing vigorously, but not just before rain, which will dilute the chemical.
THE AIM: To cover treated weeds with a fine covering of droplets.
TIP: If the spray accidentally lands on the wrong plant, wash it off straightaway with plenty of plain water. You will probably be able to save it if you work fast.

Hoeing

EFFECTIVE AGAINST: Annual and perennial weeds, including 'problem' kinds.
BEST FOR: Mass-weeding non-cluttered borders, or where plants are cultivated in straight rows, such as in vegetable beds.
WHAT TO USE: A Dutch hoe with a push-pull action, and a draw hoe with a chopping action.
WHEN TO HOE: In warm, dry weather at any time of year.
THE AIM: To slice off weed roots or uproot small seedlings while they are small. Leave them to 'fry' in the sun.
TIP: When hoeing larger weeds or if hoeing in cool damp weather, always rake up after hoeing so that weeds do not re-root.

Ready-to-use sprays

EFFECTIVE AGAINST: All weeds.
BEST FOR: Spot-treating individual perennial weeds or small patches of weeds in paving or in borders. Be sure to shield

Spot weeders

EFFECTIVE AGAINST: Perennial weeds.
BEST FOR: Treating individual weeds growing amongst other plants, or in lawns where you can't use sprays.
WHAT TO USE: A gel or aerosol formulation, or lawn weed 'stick'.
WHEN TO SPOT WEED: When weeds are growing vigorously.
THE AIM: To cover most of the leaf area with the product.
TIP: Works best on rosette weeds, such as dandelions, daisies and plantains.

Above: Some lawn spot weeders are supplied in a 'roll-on' type dispenser that you rub onto the leaves.

Left: Aerosol lawn weedkillers are intended for spot-treating individual weeds. They contain a foam 'marker' so you can see the weeds you have treated.

Watering can method

EFFECTIVE AGAINST: Annual and perennial weeds.
BEST FOR: Clearing new ground where there are no plants you want to keep.
WHAT TO USE: A contact weedkiller such as paraquat for annual weeds, or a systemic based on glyphosate where there are both annual and perennial weeds. Apply from a watering can used only for weedkiller. A dribble bar is better than a rose for quick, even application over large areas.
WHEN TO USE: When weeds are growing vigorously.
THE AIM: To cover all the foliage with a layer of fine droplets.
TIP: Do not water so heavily that the droplets run off onto the soil.

Hand weeding

EFFECTIVE AGAINST: Annual and perennial weeds.
BEST FOR: Congested borders.
WHAT TO USE: A border fork for bigger weeds or where there is more room, and a small hand fork for more detailed work.
WHEN TO HAND WEED: Easiest done when the soil is soft and moist.
THE AIM: To dig out annual weeds before they set seed. To remove all the roots of perennial weeds.
TIP: Do not put perennial weed roots on the compost heap because they regrow, with the result that you spread them all round the garden when you use your compost.

Weed prevention

The easiest way to tackle weeds is by prevention, and mulching is a much quicker option than regular hand weeding or even routine hoeing. There are two techniques. Annual mulching involves spreading a layer of organic material all over the soil between plants each spring. But for long-lasting results, cover the soil with a synthetic weed-proof membrane. You can plant through the membrane and virtually eliminate weeding altogether.

Above: A mulch usually smothers out annual weeds, but if perennial weeds poke through the mulch later on, spray them individually or dab them with glyphosate weedkiller on a brush, taking care to avoid surrounding plants. Otherwise, pull them out by hand.

Loose mulches

Most people put down a mulch around plants in spring to smother out germinating weed seedlings, but it does much more than that. A layer of material over the surface helps to 'seal' moisture into the soil so that plants don't dry out so quickly in summer. It also provides insulation for the roots of shallow-rooted plants, such as rhododendrons and perennial flowers, protecting them from overheating in summer or freezing in winter. Because the material is slowly pulled down into the soil by worms, the soil is steadily improved without you having to do any digging.

How to mulch

The best time to mulch is in early to mid-spring. The soil should be moist, well weeded and loosened with the tips of a fork before you start. Spread a 2.5-5cm (1-2in)-thick layer of the chosen mulching material between shrubs and perennials. Tuck it under overhanging branches and around the necks of plants so that all the soil is completely covered. Take care that mulches don't bury plant labels or lodge in the crowns of emerging perennials.

On light sandy soils you may need to mulch in spring and autumn. Weed seedlings can grow in the mulch once it's been on the ground for a few months, but because the mulch is loose and soft, they are very easy to pull or hoe out.

Even long-lasting mulches such as gravel will need occasional light top-ups in subsequent years, since earthworms will raise casts between the stones, which cause them to become slowly buried. With bark and gravel mulches, only a small amount of new material will be needed, but in the case of garden compost or cocoa shell mulches, you will need to renew them completely each spring.

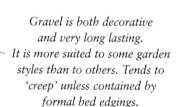

Cocoa shell is decorative and looks natural. It appears to repel slugs, snails and cats in many gardens. A slight chocolate scent is sometimes apparent when first applied. It is expensive and soon breaks down. Reapply each year.

Gravel is both decorative and very long lasting. It is more suited to some garden styles than to others. Tends to 'creep' unless contained by formal bed edgings.

Composted bark has been ground up and encouraged to partly decompose to a peat-like consistency. It does not hold as much water as peat, but is a good 'green' alternative to use when planting or if you want a very natural-looking mulch.

Bark chippings are decorative, especially in shrub or woodland gardens. They are longer-lasting than some mulches; the chunkier grades, such as these pine chippings, last five years or more. However, they are expensive and the smaller grades still need topping up annually.

SHEET MULCHES

Sheet mulches

If you want to cut down the regular chores in the garden, then permanent synthetic mulches are the answer, as they form a completely weed-proof barrier over the ground. They are usually made of perforated or woven material, so that rain and air can get through, but not weeds.

Black polythene sheeting is the cheapest material. Make holes in it once it is laid out by stabbing it at frequent intervals with a garden fork. Being thin, it tends to ruck up into folds that soon show through the covering material if you walk over the area, and it can tear.

Perforated or slitted plastic already has holes in it. It costs more, but still rucks up and tears if you need to walk over the area.

Spun landscape fabric is stronger and also more durable. It is still lightweight and needs anchoring down.

Woven 'landscape fabric' is the heaviest quality of them all and won't tear. It is expensive but worth it, as it is trouble-free.

The best time to put them down is when you are making a new bed or border for trees and shrubs. It is difficult to fit them around existing plants, and they don't work very well where you have carpets of perennials or spring bulbs. With these, you would have to leave so many gaps in the fabric for the plants to come up that weeds would get through, too. To hide the fabric, which doesn't look very attractive, spread bark chippings or gravel over it once it is down. However, since worms can't get at it, you won't need to do much topping up later.

How to use

Mark out the new bed and prepare the soil as usual. Lay anti-weed fabric over the area and hold it down securely with the special anchoring pegs sold for the purpose. Stand plants, still in their pots, on the matting while you decide where they will look best. Do any rearranging before committing yourself to cutting the mulch material. When you are happy with the arrangement, cut a cross in the fabric with scissors where you want to plant. Peel back the corners, put in the plant and then tuck the flaps of fabric back around the neck of the plant. Spread 2.5-5cm (1-2in) of bark chippings or gravel all over the bed to hide the fabric.

Laying a mulching sheet

1 *Stretch the sheet taut over well-prepared soil and skewer the edges with special 'prongs' to stop the fabric working loose and being pulled into ridges later on. Push down each prong so that the top lies flush with the soil.*

2 *Once the sheet is secured, cover it with a loose mulching material, such as bark chippings or gravel. Avoid organic mulches, such as garden compost, because airborne seeds will be able to grow in it.*

Right: *Gravel is a particularly suitable mulch in a hot sunny border planted with drought-tolerant plants. In this classic gravel garden, spiky clumps of thrift, sisyrinchium and grasses are natural partners in a dry, rocky setting.*

Pruning and trimming

Pruning is the job everyone worries about, but in practice, very few plants need much cutting back at all. Most trees and shrubs need nothing more than an occasional tidy-up to restore their shape after they are about five years old. There are a few exceptions that need regular pruning, but even then the job is usually a lot easier than you would imagine.

Remedial pruning

Dead, damaged or diseased branches – the '3 Ds'

Cut these out whenever you see them. Trim dead branches or stems back to the place where they join a healthy shoot, or to the main trunk or close to the base of the plant, whichever seems most appropriate.

Improving old or overgrown shrubs

You can do this at any time of year if you need to tidy up a neglected garden in a hurry, but ideally do it in winter or early spring just before shrubs start growing. Remove one or two of the oldest main branches as close as possible to ground level. Then shorten long or out-of-shape branches. Remove another one or two of the oldest branches in this way each year until the entire plant has been renewed. Don't cut the whole shrub back hard in one go, otherwise it will stop flowering for several years.

Shrubs that have outgrown their space

To make a garden look well-filled straightaway, you quite often find that the original plants were put in closer together than the recommended spacing. By the time they have been growing for several years, the garden becomes overcrowded. It is no good trying to prune them to keep them small. Decide which shrubs you really want to keep and then remove the rest to thin out the display and give the remaining plants more room to develop properly.

In some cases, a shrub has been planted in a small space without anyone realising how big it would grow. Regular hard pruning is not the answer, as it just stops the shrub flowering and also makes it grow back stronger than ever. The only answer is to dig it out and replace it with something more compact.

Dealing with debris

Nowadays, bonfires are considered to be antisocial, so before planting several fruit trees and bushes or roses that need plenty of regular cutting back, think about how you are going to get rid of all the prunings. Woody waste can go on the compost heap if it has been put through a shredder first, but shredders are very noisy and can often annoy neighbours as much as bonfires. You may need to take woody rubbish to a special disposal site (contact your local council). If you are clearing an overgrown garden with many plants that need cutting back, consider hiring a skip. You can use well-dried, woody prunings, cut up into suitable lengths, on a wood-burning stove. Alternatively, make good use of prunings as a source of peasticks and home-grown plant supports around the garden.

Important

Don't attempt major jobs on large trees yourself. Qualified tree surgeons have the necessary training and the correct equipment to tackle jobs that involve climbing. They can thin out trees or raise the height of the crown by removing bottom branches to let more light into a shady garden. They can also remove dangerous branches or undertake safe removal of the entire tree if that is the only option.

Removing a branch

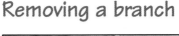

1 *When removing a large branch, use a pruning saw and start by cutting a third of the way through from beneath. The aim is to make a clean cut through the bark.*

2 *Cut the rest of the way through from above until the two cuts meet. Support the end of the branch with your free hand so that the branch does not suddenly snap off.*

3 *The branch will come away cleanly, without leaving splinters or tearing the bark, and making only a small wound that is less likely to become infected.*

WHEN TO PRUNE

Roses

Prune modern bush roses in early spring, others in summer. See page 47 for details.

Clematis

Many kinds need no regular pruning at all, but any of the vigorous, large-flowered hybrids that start blooming after early midsummer are best cut down to about 15cm (6in) above ground level early each spring. This keeps the flowers appearing at a height where you can see them, otherwise, the plants keep getting higher and only produce flowers at the top.

Spring-flowering shrubs

Shrubs such as forsythia, flowering currant (ribes) and philadelphus can be pruned immediately after they finish flowering. Cut back the branches that carried the current year's flowers to the point where they join with an unflowered branch. This keeps the bush tidy and stops it getting too big, but doesn't affect the following year's flowering.

Fruit trees and bushes

Carry out summer pruning of soft fruit bushes and blackberry canes after picking the fruit, and remove large old stems close to the base of the plant in winter.

Prune cordon apple trees and espaliers in late summer. Standard trees can usually be left without any pruning, beyond removing dead, damaged or diseased branches, unless the crown becomes congested. In this case, just remove a few whole branches to thin it out and let in more light.

Variegated trees and shrubs

Check these over each summer and remove any all-green shoots completely, as soon as you see them, as they grow faster than variegated ones and can quickly take over.

Above: It is quite common to find that some variegated plants produce green shoots. Because they grow faster than variegated shoots, they soon take over unless they are removed. Cut them right out from their base, and the plant will continue to grow as usual.

Above: If spring-flowering shrubs such as philadelphus are big and crowded with old stems, cut out a few of the weakest at ground level when you do the regular pruning. Don't cut down the whole shrub hard, as it will just grow more strongly and stop flowering.

Topiary

Clip potted topiary and trained trees growing in the garden each time the outline becomes fuzzy due to new shoots. Early and late summer are the best times to trim popular topiary subjects, such as box, which need trimming twice yearly. Use hedging shears or one-handed sheep shears.

Pruning implements

Pruning saw *Useful for branches that are too big to cut through with secateurs.*

Secateurs *For stems up to 2.5cm (1in) thick. Anvil types have a blade that cuts down onto a base plate. Bypass types have a 'parrot beak'. As long as they are clean and sharp, both give a good cut, so choose whichever you prefer. Keep an old pair for rough jobs. When using secateurs, bend the branch you are cutting away from the direction of the cut to help you get through thick branches.*

Long-handled loppers *Long-handled secateurs with bigger jaws and more leverage for tackling thicker branches. Also useful for reaching into the middle of dense old shrubs.*

Spring Essentials

Spring is the start of the growing season, and now is the time to get up to date with routine chores. Once the garden is safely under control, you can easily keep on top of the work with little more than routine maintenance for the rest of the season.

Trees, shrubs and climbers

Prune modern bush roses and those varieties of clematis that need it. Prune winter jasmine and spring-flowering shrubs as soon as the flowers are over. Weed, mulch and feed all woody plants. Use a general-purpose fertiliser, but if you have roses, then use rose feed for everything to save buying two different products.

Now is a good time to plant hardy woody plants, so that they are well established before the start of the hot, dry weather. Delay planting marginally hardy species, such as many wall shrubs, until after the last frost. They will be much better able to withstand the cold the following winter when they are properly established.

Pond

Divide any water plants that need it. Mostly, this is a job that only needs doing every five years. There's no need to empty out the water and start again. Just lift out pond plants, tip them out of their planting baskets and divide them in the same way as garden perennials (see page 39). Plant one piece back into the original basket using proper pond planting mixture. Do this early in the season, before the fish start breeding or there are tadpoles in the water. It's easier to keep frogspawn floating in the deep end while you tackle the water plants than to shake out fish fry and tadpoles later on. Do not divide water lilies until early summer.

Salad and herb bed

Fork over the soil and rake in a dressing of general-purpose fertiliser. For the earliest sowings, cover the soil with cloches or black plastic for two to three weeks to warm it up.

Sow spring onions, lettuce, radishes, parsley, dill, marjoram, chervil and coriander. Plant onion sets, shallots, garlic cloves and hardy herb plants.

Put salad potatoes to sprout in a warm dark place indoors. Plant them in mid- to late spring when the young shoots are almost 2.5cm (1in) long, putting them 7.5cm (3in) deep so that the shoots don't appear above ground while there is still any risk of frost.

Sow tomatoes on a warm windowsill indoors and prick out seedlings when their first true leaf opens out. Plant the seedlings individually in small pots of seed mixture, so that their seed leaves are barely above the surface of the mixture.

Lawn

Start mowing as soon as the grass dries out sufficiently, and redefine lawn edges with the back of a spade so that overhanging grass can be neatened with shears. Repair bare patches by reseeding them with a mixture of seed planting mix and grass seed.

Mend broken lawn edges by cutting out a square of turf and either replacing it with a new piece or by turning it round so that

Left: In early spring, use an old kitchen knife to divide overgrown clumps of plants growing at the edge of the pond, such as iris. Replant a section back into the planting basket using special aquatic soil, not potting mixture or garden soil. Spread a 2.5cm (1in)-deep layer of pebbles over the surface of the aquatic soil to stop it floating out when you put the plant back into the pond.

Left: For the earliest crops, cover the soil with cloches two weeks before sowing or planting vegetables in spring, and leave them over the row until crops fill the space.

Right: As soon as perennial plants come through the ground, place support frames over those that are likely to flop to keep the plants a compact shape.

the broken edge no longer faces the bed. Then fill the hole with potting mixture and reseed it.

If moss is a problem, treat it with moss killer and then rake it out. Delay feeding the lawn until late spring, when the worst wintry weather is past.

Hedges and fences

Clear weeds and ivy out of the bottom of the hedge and sprinkle a general-purpose fertiliser in a 30cm (12in)- wide strip along each side of the hedge.

Above: Raking out living moss is hard work and you risk spreading it. Kill it first with a moss killer and it comes out easily. Put the dead moss on the compost heap; it will soon break down, making a spongy soil improver.

Left: Repair lawns by sprinkling a mixture of seed and planting mixture over bald patches in spring. Mark the area with sticks and stones to keep pets and birds off it, and water well during spells of dry weather.

Clip fast-growing hedges every six weeks from the time they start growing, around the middle of spring until they stop growing in early autumn. Give slow-growing hedges, such as box, their first clip of the season in late spring and a second one in late summer.

Patios and containers

Clean patio slabs with a pressure washer or brush them using a stiff broom and a bucket of weak detergent in warm water. Clean containers that have been standing outdoors all winter.

When they are over, replace winter displays, such as ornamental cabbages, with spring bedding, such as coloured primroses and polyanthus or pots of spring bulbs. Choose plants that are just coming into flower and avoid disturbing the rootballs when tipping them out of their pots. Alternatively, make temporary displays by plunging pots up to their rims in old potting mixture or bark chippings, so that individual plants can be easily removed and replaced to keep the display looking its best over several months.

Beds and borders

Cut down any dead stems left from the previous year and remove any early weeds. Sprinkle general-purpose fertiliser around plants and then, while the exposed soil is moist, add a mulch, covering all the soil with 2.5-5cm (1-2in) of well-rotted compost, manure or bark chippings.

Now is a good time to put in any new perennial plants. All but the very earliest kinds will have enough time to become properly established before flowering. Leave the foliage of spring bulbs to die back naturally for at least six weeks before tidying it up.

In late spring, when the new shoots of perennials have put on some growth, push

twiggy pea sticks around airy plants, such as perennial gypsophila, for support, or place plant frames over chunkier plants, such as peony or dwarf varieties of delphiniums.

Two to three weeks before the last frost is expected, plant dahlia tubers well below the soil surface so that the young shoots remain below the ground until there is no risk to them.

Plant lily bulbs in groups of three or five. All except *Lilium candidum* should be planted at three times their own depth; leave the very tips of *L. candidum* bulbs showing just above ground level.

Above: Cocoa shell makes an attractive mulch, which some people find helps to repel slugs, snails and cats. It needs topping up every spring. Alternatively, use garden compost, which is free, or bark chippings, which last longer.

Summer
Regular maintenance

Now that all the soil preparation, clearing up and planting have been done, the main jobs you must attend to are routine mowing, weeding and watering, which need to be done regularly. Spend some time tending your flowers and enjoy being out in the garden now that the long evenings have arrived.

Beds and borders

Keep up to date with hoeing and weeding. Water newly planted perennials and put in annuals to fill odd gaps after the last frost.

Push in stakes or canes alongside tall, top-heavy plants, such as giant delphiniums or dahlias, and support individual stems by tying them up with raffia or soft string. Cut dead stems of early-flowering perennials close to the ground. If the foliage of some early perennials, such as alchemilla and pulmonaria, looks jaded, this can also be cut off close to the ground. The plants will quickly replace it with fresh, healthy foliage.

As summer moves on, deadhead large-flowered perennials regularly to keep the plants looking tidy. Regularly pick sweet peas and other flowers for cutting so the plants keep producing a new supply.

Patios and containers

As soon as the last frosts are over, replace spring bedding in tubs, troughs and windowboxes with tender patio plants, such as pelargoniums, petunias and fuchsias, for colourful summery displays.

Check containers daily and water as often as necessary to keep the potting mixture moist. If hanging baskets dry out, lift them down and stand them in a large bowl of water to soak overnight, before replacing them. As summer progresses and containers become more crowded, they will need more watering than usual; in hot weather you may need to water twice daily by midsummer.

Use diluted liquid tomato feed once a week instead of plain water to keep containers flowering well, and remove dead flowerheads regularly. With good care, the same plants should keep flowering right up to the first autumn frosts.

Shrubs and climbers

Keep new climbers tied in until they start to grip onto trellis and other supports on their own. As long as you don't break up the ball of roots when you take them out of their pots,

Left: Deadhead lupins by removing the complete stem as soon as the last flowers are over. By doing this early and feeding the plants, you may encourage a second flush of flowers, especially in a good summer when plants are growing well.

you can continue planting new trees, shrubs and climbers right through the summer, even when they are in flower or fruit. Be sure to keep them very well watered for the rest of the summer.

Regularly check roses and other grafted plants, such as witch hazel and contorted hazel, and remove any strong, straight stems

Above: When deadheading roses, cut about four leaves below the lowest bloom in the bunch. Cut the stem just above a leaf and a new flowering shoot will soon grow.

growing out of the ground close to the base of the plant. These are suckers growing from the rootstock.

Deadhead roses regularly and sprinkle a second dose of rose fertiliser around the plants in early summer to encourage further flowering. If the soil is not damp at the time, water the feed well in. Brush spilt fertiliser off the foliage of perennials to avoid scorching the leaf surfaces.

Left: Water newly planted hanging baskets to settle the potting mixture around the roots. Water every few days until the roots fill the container. At this point you may need to water baskets twice daily.

Salad and herb bed

Continue sowing lettuce, rocket, land cress, radishes and spring onions little and often to ensure a continuous supply. In midsummer, sow a mixture of oriental leaf vegetables, such as Chinese cabbage and pak choi, to use for salad leaves. These and oriental radishes are all ready to use towards the end of the season.

In early and midsummer, sow baby carrots, beetroot and kohl rabi (an unusual 'root' with crisp, pale green flesh that is good thinly sliced or grated as salad when pulled at ping-pong ball size).

Above: Leave tomatoes to ripen on the plant and only pick them when they are properly red, so that the full flavour can develop. But don't leave them on until they turn soft.

Pond

After the last frost, you can put tender floating water plants, such as water lettuce and fairy moss, out on the pond.

Regularly thin out excess water weeds and skim off floating duckweed with a small net, otherwise it can choke the pond.

Start feeding fish in early summer when they get livelier and the weather warms up. They don't really need it as there are plenty of natural midge larvae and other wild food in the pond for them, but it helps to tame them and bring them up to the surface if you feed at the same time each day. Stop feeding them at the end of summer.

Fences and hedges

To keep them looking trim, continue clipping fast-growing hedges, such as privet and *Lonicera nitida*, on a regular basis. Give slower box and yew hedges their second cut in late summer. With old-established hedges of these species, it is possible to reduce clipping to once per year, in which case this is the time to do it.

Lawn

Avoid watering the lawn unless you have to, and don't use fertilisers or lawn treatments when the weather is hot and dry, as you risk scorching the grass. Raise the mower blades in hot weather, as longer grass stays greener. Don't give up mowing entirely in dry spells, otherwise upright weeds start to invade the lawn; they can't survive regular cutting.

Try to move garden furniture around so that you don't use the same spot all the time, which wears out the grass when it isn't growing fast.

Above: Be sure to hoe regularly between rows of vegetables and salads, as weeds compete for valuable food and water. If left unchecked, they could smother your crops, resulting in a very small return.

To keep a small bed as productive as possible, clear away old leaves and debris as soon as each row of crops has been finished. Sprinkle some pelleted chicken manure over the ground and rake it in, and sow or plant the next crop straightaway. Do not let the soil in a salad bed dry out badly in summer, otherwise crops may run to seed and the roots will be tough.

Feed tomato plants every week with diluted liquid tomato feed, and remove sideshoots regularly from upright (cordon) varieties but not from bush kinds. Keep tying new growth to supports to stop the plants breaking. Wait till tomatoes are well coloured before picking them; don't be tempted to remove lower leaves to speed things up. Towards the end of the summer, nip off the tops of the plants to help any

remaining green tomatoes swell and ripen before the plants are killed by autumn frost. In late summer, sow an overwintering strain of spring onions, spinach for baby salad leaves, and an early variety of carrot. These are the fastest to mature and will be ready in autumn.

As areas of the soil are cleared of crops, dig in garden compost so that they are ready to fork over and sow early the following spring.

Deadheading Tip

Above: Use your finger and thumbnail to nip off the dead heads of bedding plants such as petunia.

To keep bedding plants flowering all summer, you must remove the dead flowerheads every week, otherwise the plants will set seed, which stops them producing new flowers.

End of season clear up

By autumn the garden is slowing down, and a new range of flowers and foliage takes over from the riotous colours of summer. It's time for a tidy-up. Winter is the best time to do any garden planning, and while there are few routine chores to take up your time, carry out landscaping work, such as paving, putting in fences or arches and preparing the ground for new beds.

Autumn

Beds and borders

When all the flowers are finished and the leaves start to turn yellow, cut perennial plants down to just above the ground if you like a very tidy garden. Otherwise, clear up weeds and leave the main tidying until the following spring. Some people prefer to put up with 'untidy' borders in winter, as the debris supports large numbers of beneficial insects, and old seedheads provide a natural source of food for birds.

Clear summer bedding from containers and replace it with ornamental cabbages and winter-flowering pansies, which start flowering now.

Gather fallen leaves from the lawn and from beds of small plants, such as rock plants, which are easily smothered. A garden vacuum cleaner is the easy way if you have many borders with tiny plant treasures.

Pile debris gathered from clearing up the garden in autumn into a compost bin. It will be ready to put back on the garden as mulching material next spring.

Salad and herb bed

Cover late crops with cloches or horticultural fleece for protection from bad weather. This way, you can extend the salad season well into autumn. Plant over-wintering onions sets to keep some of the space filled productively through the winter. They will be ready to eat in early summer the following year.

If you are an organic gardener, sow green manure crops, such as tares and winter rye, on vacant spaces in late summer and autumn. This is a valuable technique for improving the soil naturally. Dig in green

Above: Overwintering onion sets can be planted 5-7.5cm (2-3in) apart and will be ready to pull in early summer. They don't store for long, so use them immediately and sow or plant something else in the space straightaway.

Left: A layer of fallen leaves will prevent the light reaching the lawn, making it turn yellow and prone to fungal disease. Rake up the leaves and turn them into leafmould (see page 76) for improving the soil or making potting compost.

manure crops early the following spring. Six weeks later they have decomposed, leaving the ground ready for sowing or planting.

Trees, shrubs and climbers

Autumn is the very best time to plant woody plants, such as trees and shrubs. Plant or move evergreens in early autumn for best results. They will all be well established by the following summer, so they will not need watering, unlike plants put in during the growing season.

Lawn

Give lawns a low-nitrogen autumn/winter feed to encourage root growth. It won't make any extra mowing, as it doesn't cause lush leafy growth.

Older, heavily used lawns need extra help to recover from wear. Rake out any moss, and when the soil is moist, slit or spike the turf using a garden fork pushed in every 10-15cm (4-6in) to spike the lawn, or use a mechanical lawn aerator. (Powered grass slashers can sometimes be hired by the day or for a weekend.) Then brush coarse horticultural sand into the surface, so that some trickles down the holes and forms drainage channels. Follow with an application of autumn lawn feed.

Above: Spiking reduces the effects of compaction on a lawn. Do it every autumn in places that get heavy use. Sprinkle sharp sand over the area afterwards and brush it well in.

Above: Putting a taut net over your pond keeps dead leaves out of the water and protects fish from predators.

Prepare the ground for new lawns. Early autumn is the best time to sow grass seed, as you will have a good lawn by spring. Lay turf at any time from autumn to spring, except when the soil is unworkable due to bad weather.

Pond

Stop feeding fish when the weather turns cold. Cut back marginal plants around the water's edge. Regularly remove fallen leaves with a small fishing net or cover the pond with netting until the following spring to stop them blowing into the water. This also deters herons from taking your fish.

Winter

Tree stump removal

If access is too limited to have old stumps winched out and they are too big to dig up, hire a stump grinder to remove tree stumps and their roots. A stump grinder reduces the stump to sawdust; shovel this out and replace it with topsoil. Then you can plant something else in the spot straightaway.

Pruning

Prune standard apple and pear trees. Don't snip at twigs around the edge; remove entire branches growing into the centre of the crown to let in more light and thin out overcrowded branches. Remove the 3 Ds – dead, damaged or diseased branches. Cherries, plums and other fruit trees are best left alone. Prune trained trees, such as fans or cordons, in summer.

Pond

If you have fish, don't let a solid sheet of ice remain over the pond for more than 12 hours. Use a hot saucepan to melt a hole to let in air – don't smash it with a hammer.

Insulating containers

Protect planted winter containers from long spells of freezing weather by lagging them with insulation material and covering plants with horticultural fleece. Alternatively, move them temporarily under cover into a shed or carport.

Below: If the potting mix freezes solid, plants in containers can die from lack of water, so lag patio plants before they freeze solid.

Index

Credits

The publishers would like to thank the following photographers for providing images, credited here by page number and position: B(Bottom), T(Top), C(Centre), BL(Bottom Left), etc.

© Bookmart Publishing: 12(BL, BR), 13(T), 17(B), 25(TR, C, B), 33, 38(TR), 44(T), 45(BC), 48(C, BR), 66(CR, BL, BC, BR), 69(TC, TR, C, CR), 71(TL), 75(TC, B), 77(TC), 82(TR), 86(BL, BR), 86-7(T), 87(TR, CL), 88(BL), 89(TR), 90(CR), 91(T)

Geoffrey Rogers: © Bookmart Publishing: 11(C, B), 12(C), 13(B), 15(CL), 22(B), 28(L), 32(C), 33(B), 37(BC, BR), 39(TR), 42(TR, BC), 46(B), 49(TR, BL), 51(C, B), 63, 67(T), 74(TC), 78(L), 80(BR), 82(BL), 83(CL), 85(TR), 87(BR), 88-89(T), 91(BL)

Neil Sutherland © Bookmart Publishing: 5, 14(T), 15(C, CR), 16(TL), 20(BL, CR), 21, 28(C), 29, 32(BL), 33(T), 43, 44(CL, BC, BR), 53, 55, 56(CL, BL), 57(CL, C, BL, BR), 58(C), 59, 61(TC, TR, BC, BR), 65(BL, BR), 70(TR), 76(CL), 80-81(T), 81, 83(CT, CB), 85(B), 86(BR), 88(CR), 89(BR)

Dave Bevan: 10(C), 47(T), 56-57(T), 74(TL, C), 75(TL), 76(BL), 78(BR), 78-79(B), 79(T, C, CR), 80(CL)

Eric Crichton: 3, 14(B), 18(Chiffchaffs), 19(CR), 19(B Coles Garden) 22(TL Pembroke Hort. Soc.), 30(Mortimore), 31(CR Copeland), 32(BR), 34(TL), 34-35(T), 35(TR, B), 36(CR), 37(TR), 44(BL), 49(CR), 54(TR, Foulsham), 57(TR), 58(TR, B), 60(CR), 61(BL), 62(C), 68(T, Sinclair), 74(BC), 83(BR)

John Glover: 2(C), 4(Parham, Sussex), 9, 19(T, Designer Bunny Guinness), 20(T), 22(TR, Nash Fuchsias), 23(CR, Camden Hill Square, London), 24, 31(BR, Great Dixter, Sussex), 32(TR), 34(B), 39(B), 41(B, The Manor House, Chenies, Bucks.), 42(CL, BR), 49(TL, Upper Woodhill Farm, Surrey), 50(BL), 50(BC, Whichford Pottery, Warwickshire), 51(TR, Colgrove Seeds, Oxon), 52(C, BR), 54(BL), 60(TR), 62-63(T), 63(TR), 64(L), 66-67(T, Shenley Ave., Shropshire), 68(BR, The Mill House, Essex), 71(CL, Designer Julian Dowle), 75(CL), 76(CR, Heligan, Cornwall), 77(CL, The Anchorage, Kent), 90(B), 91(BR)

S & O Mathews: 2(R), 6-7, 15(BR), 26-27(The Old Vicarage, Edington), 31(BL), 35(CR), 37(TL), 40(BL), 45(TR), 46(CL), 47(BL), 48(TR), 52(CL, BC), 54(C), 64(C), 65(TL, CR), 68(C), 69(BL), 70(TL, BR), 71(C), 72-73, 78(CR)

Peter J May: 17(TR), 28(TR), 77(BR), 84(BL, BC, BR), 85(C), 89(C)

Clive Nichols Garden Pictures: Half title page (The Nichols Garden, Reading), 23(B, Designer Clare Matthews), 40(BR), 41(TR), 46(TR, Guy Farthing), 49(BR), 60(BL)

Geoffrey Rogers: 2(B), 11(TL), 13(B), 38(BL, CB, CR), 39(C), 40-41(T), 41(CR), 51(TL)

Eric Sawford: 23(CL, Agriframes), 36(B), 45(C)

The artwork illustrations have been prepared by Stuart Watkinson and are © Bookmart Publishing.

Additional design layout by Phil Holmes.

Acknowledgements

The publishers would like to thank the following people and organisations for their help during the preparation of this book: Richard Phillips and the staff at Russells Garden Centre, Birdham, West Sussex for providing facilities for photography; Millbrook Garden Centre, Northfleet, Kent; Murrells Nursery, Pulborough, West Sussex.